Going Through Life with a "Kick Me" Sign

Going Through Life With a "Kick Me" Sign

The Story of an Urban Educator

Harry Lee

iUniverse

GOING THROUGH LIFE WITH A "KICK ME" SIGN
THE STORY OF AN URBAN EDUCATOR

iUniverse books may be ordered through booksellers or by contacting:

iUniverse
1663 Liberty Drive
Bloomington, IN 47403
www.iuniverse.com
1-800-Authors (1-800-288-4677)

Because of the dynamic nature of the Internet, any web addresses or links contained in this book may have changed since publication and may no longer be valid. The views expressed in this work are solely those of the author and do not necessarily reflect the views of the publisher, and the publisher hereby disclaims any responsibility for them.

Any people depicted in stock imagery provided by Thinkstock are models, and such images are being used for illustrative purposes only.
Certain stock imagery © Thinkstock.

ISBN: 978-1-4917-6965-2 (sc)
ISBN: 978-1-4917-6964-5 (e)

Library of Congress Control Number: 2015910619

Print information available on the last page.

iUniverse rev. date: 7/22/2015

DEDICATIONS

I would like to take a few moments to mention and thank some very important people in my life who have in some way made this collection of experiences and memories a reality.

First, I want to thank God for his mercy and grace. His support was my strength. He always had things in control, even when I didn't know it.

I want to thank my wife. She is the best partner for the journey of life. Her smile and laughter touched my heart from the day I first met her. She keeps life interesting and every day is something different. She has given me a second chance at love and provides it unconditionally.

My two kids are the pride of my life. They survived the divorce fairly well, and are successful married young adults, college graduates in the working world. You make me proud that I am your dad.

Thanks to my parents. Their example to me is my guiding light in how to be a responsible parent and adult in this world. I am fortunate they are still around and healthy. I treasure the time we have together.

My sister and brother. They are part of who I am. Both have helped my life along the way, and my sister was a strength during the early onset of depression.

My two aunts and uncle who blazed the trail for me in education.

They were two good examples of what the good side of education can be. Thanks for your examples and encouragement.

My pastor and dear friend. His unwavering focus on God and his encouragement to me to do the same has straightened me out more than a few times. His spiritual counsel, his joining me in prayers, his support of my life, has proven to me what a real pastor is as well as a good friend. Thanks.

My buddy George. What can I say? Your friendship to this day and thru some of the most difficult days of my journey is priceless. My sincere thanks.

To all the colleagues I have had in my career. Many of you were dear acquaintances who provided a strong network of support that kept me going. A special mention to the Captain. Thanks for your wise counsel and ear to listen. You are a good man.

Dr. P- your compassion and insight helped pull me out of the dangerous time I was experiencing and point me on the road of recovery. Thank you.

Finally, to all my golfing buddies, especially Dean, Ken, and Brad. Thanks for the great rounds of fun and listening to all my stories.

I would like to list the names of those who have crossed my path in the career of teaching and left a solid impression. They are: Pearl, Donna, Bob, Joe, Bruce, Sandy, George, Ruth, Bob, Frank, Tom, T, Ron, Kellie, Vince, Ryan, Thom, Guy, Ellyn, Bags, Karen, Bill, Captain, Sue, and so many more. My sincere apologies to any I forgot. Middle age and depression can affect the memory unfortunately.

Contents

Introduction ix

Chapter 1   The Beginning. . .Literally 1

Chapter 2   The Early Days 3

Chapter 3   Early Experience in Urban Education 5

Chapter 4   Growing Up/The Younger Years 7

Chapter 5   Early School Memories 13

Chapter 6   More College Education and Preparation 16

Chapter 7   Intern Snippets and First Year Memories 18

Chapter 8   My First Class 20

Chapter 9   The Urban Chaos Begins 25

Chapter 10   The Blackboard Jungle 26

Chapter 11   The Teacher Becomes a Store Owner –
             An Attempt at Freedom 38

Chapter 12   The Blackboard Jungle – Elementary
             School – How Bad Can It Really Be? 41

Chapter 13   Interview with My Next District
             Assignment – Coming Home 57

Chapter 14   Fifth Grade Wing – Good Times, Good
             Memories 60

Chapter 15   One of the Rare Great Ones 66

Chapter 16   9/11 Terror and the Darkness 67

Chapter 17   Finally, a Chance to Be Creative 71

Chapter 18   Health Class 73

Chapter 19   The Kick Me Sign Falls Off – For a
Moment – I Find Love 81

Chapter 20   Move to a New Elementary Building and
the Alternative World.. 83

Chapter 21   New Assignment, New Principal, Final Straw...... 86

Chapter 22   5th Grade Again – A Different World 88

Chapter 23   Kick Me Sign Tries Again – A Big Scare for Me.... 92

Chapter 24   My Last Building Assignment –
Impending Doom 96

Chapter 25   Tragedy Strikes Again.. 103

Chapter 26   My Final Straw – The Breaking Point is Here..... 104

Chapter 27   My First Trip to a Psychiatrist 107

Chapter 28   Following the Yellow Brick Road 108

Chapter 29   Dealing with the STRS and Their Process............110

Chapter 30   The Moment of Truth – Meeting the
STRS Doctor...112

Chapter 31   The Crazy Ride Slows Down and Comes
to an End 114

Chapter 32   The Kick Me Sign Gets One Last Boot –
By the Union 116

Chapter 33   Depression..119

Chapter 34   Reflections, a Career Statement, and a
Little Advice... 121

Chapter 35   Epilogue – Did the Kick Me Sign Win? 124

Before I Go 127

Afterword 129

Introduction

Most people upon reaching adult age tend to look around and realize it's time to make a plan for what to do with their life. Some choose a program in a college that hopefully will capitalize on their skills and interests. It is their hope that the career will provide a chance to enjoy their profession and provide a decent living for themselves and family. Sometimes, the choices are great; others misinformed and idealistic. It is a "roll of the dice" to see what your life journey ends up being. I chose the route of educator. Later in life, I went back to complete my master's degree in hopes of finishing my career as an administrator. As a young man, I was idealistic, and knew that I was going to impact the lives of children. To an extent, I was able to do that. I had no idea at the time what this career choice would hold for me. The result, along with some major events and influences in my life, tells a story of challenges, victories, disappointments, and experiences that have certainly provided an interesting life so far. Within the pages of this book you will find a story of a man from the beginning of his life, details of his youth, adult life, and his career from beginning to retirement. Along the way you will find some humor, some interesting details, the ups and downs of an educator life in an urban setting, faith, and hopefully some inspiration to continue your journey. Life is an awesome, challenging ride; but it is worth every day of it. Enjoy the read.

CHAPTER 1
THE BEGINNING. . .LITERALLY

He was a young man growing up in a little community in the Midwest in the 50's. His dad walked out on him and his mom when he was two years old. Eventually, his mom met and married his step-dad some years later and proceeded to have four more kids with him. While not a violent man, his step-dad was a bit distant. Non-emotional, he did his best for the young man, but decided never to give him his last name or really treat him as one of his own. The step-dad provided the basic necessities of life for which the young man was grateful. The young man's half siblings always looked to him as their older brother. The reality that his biological father never cared enough to keep in touch or support him was a wound that he carried throughout his life. When it came time for him to graduate high school, he was never offered a chance at college. He was encouraged to go into the service. His siblings were granted college opportunities upon their graduation, and all had professional careers. Needless to say, he was a bit lonely, and looking for affection to give him a sense of belonging. The young man found it in a young woman who had oddly a very similar background. Their story was about to change.

She was a young, beautiful woman growing up in a similar community. Her dad divorced her natural mom at a very early age. She had seven siblings from this marriage of her dad. He went on to meet a lady some years later and had four kids with her. Although the siblings maintained civil interactions, the age difference and the two marriages always provided a bit of a challenge in normalcy. Her dad became violent towards her and her siblings. She was never allowed to maintain a relationship with her mother, who had remarried and moved away a few hours. Her step-mom was not affectionate towards her and her siblings from that marriage. The fact that her mom was unavailable to her became a wound she carried around in her life as well. Along the way, she met the young man. As often is the case in life, their backgrounds provided some common experiences that allowed them to bond and care for each other. She was approaching graduation. He was leaving for the military. You see, these are my parents, it was the summer of 1959, and this was my beginning.

CHAPTER 2
THE EARLY DAYS

This era in time maintained a morals standard in a lot of areas. One, the idea of a woman pregnant without the bond of marriage was highly frowned upon, which was viewed as the equivalent of the scarlet letter. Her already violent father and cold step mother became unbearable towards her. They felt she had to be shipped to a nun's covenant to avoid shame for herself and her family. Five months into the pregnancy the young man and she were married and in doing so got rid of the scarlet letter. During her time in the convent, continual pressure was placed on her to give me up for adoption. My mother, God love her, was a strong woman and refused. Four months later, in late July, 9lb.9 ½ oz. 22 in. long baby Harry was born. My dad was stationed in Germany. He had no leave built up as of yet. He was told the news and came home to support his wife and meet his new son as soon as he could. A few days shy of 1 year old, my dad arrived. The story is he held me in his hands at arm's length and said hello to his baby boy. The young couple, 19 and 20 yrs. old began their journey with their baby boy.

The purpose of this story is multi-faceted. It is designed to provide a look into the urban education environment to those who may be interested and yet not familiar. It is written for those already in urban environments as a way of showing a colleague's experiences so that you may feel not alone. It is a story for those who are struggling in the school systems of the inner-city to perhaps suggest some ways of making your working day a bit easier. Finally, it is written for those who are considering a career in urban education. I wished someone had been truthful with me before I made the decision to enter this specific part of education. It is also a story that invites you into the many details and life experiences of the author with the hope that in doing so you will find a collegiality that causes the education career details to be vivid and relative, to where you will understand the reason behind the title: Going through Life with a "Kick Me" Sign. The next chapter was inserted at this point to give an example of this correlation early on.

CHAPTER 3

EARLY EXPERIENCE IN URBAN EDUCATION

Fast forwarding, the scene took place in the office of an inner-city elementary school. Upon arriving for one of my first days as an observer, I accompanied my mentor teacher to observe discipline procedure in this building. It seems a chronic problem maker had been caught again. They had progressed with his discipline to the point that they either were going to paddle him or suspend him. He was clearly an angry young guy who was in the eighth grade. The paddle appeared to be a flexible leather type which gave a different impact. At this point in time, as a young, naïve student teacher I hadn't formed an opinion on if I supported such action. The student was told to put his hands on the desk and quickly was swatted twice. It was at the end of the day, and the kid stormed out of the office onto the sidewalk. He was clearly embarrassed, angry, and hurt. The look in his eyes stuck with me for quite a while. It didn't make me form an opinion either way, but certainly caused me to think.

Prior to this experience, I was enrolled in the newest program for student teacher education in a nearby university. While maintaining a full classroom load, the program provided an opportunity to work for an entire school year at three different grade levels as a student teacher in a nearby urban school district. This gave me exposure to three different teachers at three different grade levels to gain useful experience from their careers of teaching rather than the standard nine week assignment of student teaching. It was very cutting edge at the time. Along with standard observation hours, there was gradual implementation of responsibilities related to teaching given to the student teacher as time progressed. As a result, I took 54 semester hours of class in one year while working full time in the public school system, and driving 90 miles round trip on a daily basis. To say the least, while invaluable experience was attained, it was a challenge to accomplish without running myself into exhaustion.

At the first school, I had the pleasure of being mentored by a bright, veteran teacher named Dave. He had a great sense of humor, relaxed, and practical in the classroom as well as with student relations. In his class, I had my first student vomit experience. I was sitting in the back and a young man had his head down on his desk which was unusual. Dave was keeping an eye on him and knew this was not the norm. Suddenly, the kid sits up wide- eyed and lets fly all over the aisle. What was Dave's response after sending the kid to the bathroom and the nurse? He called on the intercom to the office to announce there was a clean-up needed in aisle two of room 125! I also watched and learned how to handle a volatile situation when a bully male parent came in the building at dismissal and started screaming at a female teacher. Dave eased his way between the two, smiling as always, and quietly told the guy that he can't be screaming like this in front of the kids and let's take a walk to the office to chat some more. It settled things immediately.

Finally, I noticed another male teacher. He was a burly, bearded, walrus kind of guy. Every day at the same time (which later I found was his planning period) he would go to his empty room. He would lock the door, turn out the lights, and pull a shade down over the window in his door. Curious, I snuck to his door one day to peer in. He had a reclining chair in his room, fully extended, with a timer set to go off at the end of his period. At the beep, he would get up, turn the lights on, open the door and commence teaching the next class! My kind of guy! Several years later, I attempted the same action in my own classroom in a different school system. I was approached by my principal, questioned, (I assured him it was only during planning time that it was used) to which he politely told me I had to get rid of it. Oh the politics. Too young to know better, I dispatched my beat up recliner to the waste receptacle outside. My introduction to the world of urban education had begun. I had no idea of the experiences that awaited me.

CHAPTER 4

GROWING UP/
THE YOUNGER YEARS

The first few years were spent with mom and me living on the outskirts of town, in a little upstairs apartment. She had very little help from family, although my dad was there financially from the beginning; sending home money from his Army paychecks until he honorably discharged and joined us. At approximately two years of age, my parents had a bit of a scare. They had noticed that my head appeared a bit large for my body. Being young, they did what any parent should do and took me to the pediatrician. He referred me to the world renowned hospital in our state. Upon initial observation, they felt I had been born with hydrocephalus also known as water on the brain. This condition would eventually leave me with a shunt in my brain and developmentally handicapped for life. Certainly, my young parents initially recoiled in shock. My mom has always had a faith in God, and began to ask him for intervention. After much testing, doctors came to my parents with shocking news of their own. It seems that the results indicated in their words, "Nature had corrected itself." The hydrocephalus was gone. The doctors were stunned. My parents, at that time and myself later when I was old enough to know, believed that God had seen fit to heal my body. You see, it seems he has had a plan for me since birth for my life.

We moved into the housing projects of this little town early in my life, somewhere around the age of five or six. My parents were hard working folks, blue collar workers with a great work ethic and a belief in the family being a tight core united in life. By now, I had a baby brother who was three years younger than I. I never knew the housing projects were considered to be where the "poor" people of town lived. There were a series of "blocks" that were in a U shape containing little box houses on both sides of a blacktop drive running through the center of them. These box size homes were two sides, an A and a B. In the early days, we could only afford living on one end. A small kitchen, small living room, one bathroom, and two bedrooms made up one end. My brother and I slept on bunk beds and shared a small room about 10 by 12, also sharing one closet. In the earliest location, one of my early "project" lessons occurred. Here are the details:

I was a soft-hearted kid, a little sheltered, since my parents wanted to protect me from any possible damage that could rise from having had the "corrected" case of hydrocephalus as an infant. A kid on the block, named David, was always trying to bully me. I didn't fight back. One day, I came home whimpering how he had picked on me again. My mom, having had enough, decided a little tough love would be in order. We had a fence with a locking gate on our property. She told me to go out, find David, and stick up for myself, or she wouldn't let me back in. I was scared, but knew she meant business. I went out of the gate, putting my best mean face on, calling him out. We squared off. He had a sneer on his face, thinking this was going to be an easy one. We began facing off like two boxers, putting up our hands. All of a sudden, an adrenaline rush hit, and I balled up my fist, reached way back, and punched him in the jaw. He took off running and we never had an issue again. Needless to say, mom opened the gate, and I returned the conquering hero.

Time passed, and we moved to another block, where we would stay until getting out of the projects after I graduated high school. My parents were doing a little better, and eventually were able to buy both ends of the box house to where we had moved. On this block, there were quite a few more "project" lessons that occurred. Here is a short version of some:

A Projects Education

It was here that I found out one of the expectations of being the oldest brother is the requirement of defending him against older kids that wanted to fight him. I can think of three specific occasions, but one definitely stands out in my mind. The guy's name was Willie. He was a brute. This is a guy you wouldn't want to engage in a fight. One day, I looked out to see him charging down the lane after my brother. "Oh crap" I thought, "thanks a lot little bro." I went bounding out the door, hollering for Willie to stop. My brother went in the house and I told the big guy he was going to have to fight me, because he was not getting to my brother. He grinned, and said "Okay." This was not the answer I had hoped for. We squared off boxer style, throwing out some jabs, none doing much damage. Suddenly, I felt the impact of a big right hand that he had landed square on my jaw. The world was spinning, and I thought "man, I am in trouble." Somehow, managing to remain upright, I continued throwing a few more jabs making some contact. Without warning, perhaps divine intervention, Willie just dropped his hands and said "aw forget it." As he walked away, although my chest was puffed out for the neighborhood kids to see, inside I was so happy he left before I would have hit the dirt!

About thirty years later, he and I ran into each other at a golf league opening day. We shook hands and I reminded him about the good old days when he almost broke my jaw. A good natured grin on his face, we laughed at what a small world it is as we teed off on the first hole.

More Life Lessons in the Project

On this block, there were three families of kids that each had siblings. We all grew up together playing sports frequently in the field behind our house. One family was all girls and one boy. The other family was all boys and one girl. The third was my brother and I. Our sister was born when I was 8, and my brother 3. Of course, there were times when a family would team up against another and have feuds. Typically, they didn't last long and weren't that physical. I now want to share with you a story about a mom that ruled her kingdom:

She was the mom of the family of all girls and one son. Her house was the last on the U shaped block. This woman ruled her house and that area of the block. She could sit on the porch and bellow and everybody would scramble. You just didn't make Rosy mad. Why the name Rosy? Well, she had red hair. Hey, we were kids, that's all we could come up with. One day, my brother, who was known to be pretty reckless and not fearful of injury, was riding his bicycle from up the project down towards our block on the main street that cut through the project. He had picked up some speed when he made his cut into the U shaped block right in front of this lady's house. At the end of each U shaped block there was a parking lot for folks to park who didn't have a driveway of their own, or had company. Well, my kid brother hit the gravel in that parking lot and lost control, wrecking into the side view mirror of the car parked there. As it busted off, the point behind it struck my brother in the temple area and the blood began to flow. He jumped up and was scared! No, not of the blood, but of the idea that Rosy would be coming out to get him. All I could see was his backside as he ran home for safety.

While I am at it about my brother, there was another bloody story of interest. Everyone remembers the film "The Christmas Story." In the film, one of the famous scenes was of the little kid sticking his tongue to the frozen pole. Well, guess who decided to create that scene in our yard? My brother stopped on our side porch which had aluminum railing on it and decided he was going to stick his tongue on the railing, he wasn't afraid! I ran around the corner, fearful of once again seeing the disaster. Suddenly a loud moan was heard, and around the corner he came, blood oozing out of his mouth. He never attempted to recreate that stunt again!

A Game of Pickle

One day, my sister had to be about 6, wanted to join my brother and I while we were tossing the baseball back and forth in the field. We told her okay, but only if we played pickle and she had to be it. She was thrilled. She began to run back and forth between us and the game was picking up speed. Suddenly, one of us threw the ball to the other and struck our sister in the back of the head and down she went. She was briefly knocked out. We panicked. We talked about leaving her under one of the pine trees thinking mom and dad wouldn't find her. Can you imagine? She quickly woke up while this inane discussion was happening. We didn't think like we do now with head injuries and so forth. We just told her to not tell our parents or she would never play with us again. To this day, we tease her because she has a flat spot on the back of her head that we attribute to this beaning.

Mom Gets Angry

Finally, one day my dad had taken the three of us across town to the city park to play. I was in a little league baseball game. My brother and sister played on the nearby playground equipment while my dad watched the game. In those days, no fear of any evil people existed in our small town. After the game, as we headed to the car, my brother jumped in and off we went. We were busy talking about the game and arrived home. As we walked into the house, my mom, who had been cleaning the house and making dinner, looked up and said "where is your daughter?" My dad's face turned white. He had left her at the park playground! All of us ran to the car, jumped in and raced to the park. As we pulled up, there she was playing on the swings having fun. Thank God! My dad scooped her up and my mom didn't let up on him for a long time.

My parents always had a clean house that was maintained attractively. The yard was taken care of, there was food in the fridge, and the bills were paid. How was I to know that this was considered the poor section of town? Later, I will share a bit as to how this affected my brother unknown to me till many years later in life. I attended kindergarten in a church building, having class in their Sunday school rooms. My teacher, a dear lady that reminded everyone of a grandma, did a great job with her students. I learned to enjoy school. Sadly, later on in life, this lady's husband was murdered in the woods of a nearby state park. She didn't deserve for that to happen to her husband and her life. Primary school was grades 1-3 in the elementary building in town, 4th grade in a utility building of a catholic church across town, then moving for 5th-8th in the junior high part of the high school building uptown; where we moved next door to complete high school and graduate. Fast forward many years, a major tornado struck this little town. The high school, junior high, and eventually middle school, were destroyed. It is an odd experience to take your kids for a ride thru town to see where you attended school and explaining to them where it was located, now gone from the tornado effects. It is kind of a shame that all I have is my memory rather than a chance to roam those halls again as an adult. When I turned 8, we added one more to our fold, my baby sister. The three of us began our journey of going thru this little school system till we graduated. My sister had a slight deviation in her plan; suffice it to say she ended up graduating from another little school in the area after my parents decided to move us there.

Chapter 5

Early School Memories

Parents and teachers reading this book, please take note. There is no doubt that a traumatic experience for a kid can stick with them thru life, or at least for a very long time. In 1st grade, a substitute teacher, a frightening scary woman who all of us have seen at one time or another, did something that embarrassed and stuck with me for a long time. At that age, kids were being taught how to print on paper. This is difficult enough. Then, at some point the teacher would call them to the board to recreate what they had been learning. This, for kids like me, who don't like being watched when I am trying something difficult involving dexterity, proved a nightmare. This older, harsh, rough edged lady verbally destroyed me in front of the class because I was unable to print the small letter r in the fashion required without going off the line. She began to yell, tell me start over. My hand began to shake, and it got worse to where she just said "oh forget it, go sit down." Kids had laughed; I was at the point of tears. From that day on, I never wanted to be at the board alone. I would make excuses not to be. This stayed with me into adult life, whenever similar things would occur. I remember being at a ball game with my dad who sent me to the stand for two sodas in a tall cup. They were very full with ice. I turned, began to return to him, became overwhelmed and began to shake, spilling a good part of the drinks. I remembered this incident all thru my teaching career; being careful never to put a kid into an embarrassing situation that could stick with them as that did with me.

Imagine

We actually had a milk machine in our elementary building that would dispense ½ pints of milk, white and chocolate, for 3 cents. Can you imagine? This was in the early to mid-sixties.

Some Elementary School Memories

Third grade: the grade I first developed an interest in performing in front of the class, (no chalk and chalkboard) Bill Cosby was big at this time. My dad had an album of his (for you young people, not a photo album, but a vinyl record album) that we listen and laughed to at home. I rehearsed one of his skits (Noah and the Lord) and would show off in front of the class when Mrs. Hill would allow it.

Sixth grade: we had a very strict male teacher for the first time. Kids who have never experienced a male teacher before have to adjust to a new way the teacher runs the class. Males tend to be a little more non-nurturing as the ladies do. His class was run with more of rules, structure, manners, and following directions with respect. Well needless to say, kids rebel at times. We had paddling back then, so it was nothing for him to administer corporal punishment when he had enough of our nonsense. When he would stand at the board to teach with his back to us, Norm liked to stand and give him the finger to the chuckles of the classmates. At the end of the year, he asked us to write an essay, sharing the good and the bad so that he could improve his style for next year. I was raised in a family that attended church and didn't approve of swearing. My first act of rebellion was that at the end of my essay, I boldly printed "in other words Mr. D. this past year has been HELL!" I thought surely I would be in trouble by the time I got home. I forgot the reason why I was so emboldened to do this manly gesture. *He didn't make us put our names on it....*

Embarrassment and Disappointment

One of the more humiliating things I went thru in life was in trying to play sports that involved helmets, there was never one that could fit me properly. In this day and age, that would necessitate the school purchasing one to do the job. I overheard my two simpleton coaches in 8th grade talking and wondering what they were going to do about a helmet? The one said "I don't know, have you seen the size of his head?"

One other difficult incident comes to mind in high school. I had been a member of National Honor Society since junior year, and it was time to graduate. I received no credit for my accomplishments or service for two years. It seems my GPA upon graduation had slipped from 3.0 to 2.975. For .025 points I had been removed. Later in life, I had this crop up again with my son's school. He had worked hard, and was well known and liked by all. He graduated 8th in his class and yet, he didn't qualify for National Honor Society! I went full bore to the superintendent who offered weak excuses. I found that membership comes down to it being more of a social club vs. an academics club in some schools. Apparently, a random individual did not give their approval so therefore he was denied. Seems like the ol' kick me sign was around my neck for quite a while before my career even started.

Let's look at some of the early experiences I had in teacher education before being sent out to the blackboard jungle.

CHAPTER 6

MORE COLLEGE EDUCATION AND PREPARATION

When we last looked at this item, I had taken you into the first school I had experience in as a student teacher in the university internship program. Prior to this year, I had to work part-time while going to school part-time for about seven years. My parents were not in a position to pay for my education, and at the time student loans really weren't as popular as they were today. Along the way, I met a woman who I dated for a while, who later became my wife and the mother of my two children. We were part of a church which wasn't exactly your "normal" type of church. We believed in God, Jesus, the Bible, but outside of that a lot of what we learned was interpreted by the preacher who had unchecked power. I was always raised that the man should be the primary breadwinner of the home. Therefore, part time work and part time school had to come to an end since she was working full time. For one year, I took 53 semester hours of class along with working the school year in three different locations in an urban district. While a definite opportunity to experience a lot more than the standard student teaching experience, it was exhausting. During this time, my classes were also at main campus. This meant a daily commute round trip of about 100 miles. I graduated in August of 1985 on a Friday. I was in my classroom that next Monday. Did I mention that it was 160 mile round trip for $14,000? I couldn't afford a good enough car to sustain the journey, so I went thru four of them in that first year. At the time, all I cared about was I was full time working in my own class. Logic should have dictated that I take a year and work as a sub in numerous locations, getting my name and reputation out there so I could get a spot locally. Sadly, logic wasn't my strong suit at that time, and I made the choice that I did. One last thing, two weeks after starting my first classroom position my first child was born. Life sure had begun to change.

Chapter 7

Intern Snippets and First Year Memories

One of my first assignments in this internship program was to work with a 1st grade class, whose teacher's name was Molly. There was some concern since I had no interest in the little ones as far as my career choice, but since the degree was grades 1-8, a little experience was in order. If you have never witnessed the skill it takes to work a group of 5 and 6 year olds in a classroom with order, it truly is a treat. Always a smile, warm but firm, she showed me how it works. One of my highlights was the simple task of reading a book to the class in a way to keep them involved. It really turned out to be fun. One of my most embarrassing moments was when asked to change the bulletin board, I began with enthusiasm. I mean, how hard can this be, right? A few minutes into it I found out when I managed to staple my finger. By the grace of God, I didn't lose it, just yelped a bit. There is nothing better than a group of innocent little ones all worried that "the big teacher" was hurt. Working with Molly was my pleasure, a true talent.

I had another assignment that showed me what happens when paired with someone who really isn't there for you, but more to give you lots of her work and be hypercritical. Not fun!

Recess was fun when I worked with the 4th thru 6th grade kids and I was able to play football and kickball with them. I also learned it can be a dangerous place. One day, as I walked outside from the building door, I approached a corner where I was ready to walk out from the building into the clear of the playground. At the exact same moment, a 5th grader had unleashed a baseball pass of a basketball to a friend across the court which struck me flush in the side of the head and face. I saw stars and thought I was going to pass out. I shook it off, (after all who wants to show kids that you can't take a hit!) and went about my day. I always remembered from that point on to come out from a side wall of a building carefully so as to never get pasted again.

In its totality, the internship program was the best thing going at the time to prepare for the real world of teaching. Classwork, book learning, was a necessary evil, and gave some rudimentary basics by which to navigate your teaching day.

A Small bit of Advice

In honesty, I believe that teachers are not taught how to teach, they are born that way. You either are or you aren't. You should know relatively quick which one is you. If you aren't, don't stick around. If you are, learn fast, and begin to affect the kids' lives that you have been assigned. It takes a long time to reach a pay level that is decent. There are days where you wonder who you are, and if you can take it anymore. At the end of the day, if you can honestly say that the kids keep you going, then stick around. You are about to go on a career journey that will provide memories, both good and bad, that will last a life time.

I hope to give you little glimpses thru my experiences of some of what you can expect. I was getting ready to enter the blackboard jungle. Little did I know what was waiting to greet me.

Chapter 8

My First Class

As I mentioned a bit earlier, I graduated in August 1985, on a Friday. My first day of class was the following Monday. Talk about being thrown in the deep end and told learn how to swim! Here I was, ready to splash. The trip was 80 miles one way. It was a small suburban/rural school system in an elementary 4th grade classroom. I was assigned 20+ kids. It was a small staff. It was run by a principal who I later found out had control issues in my opinion. I had the privilege of having two super teacher neighbors across the hall, Pam and Dawn, who were my life savers. Pam helped me with some of the teaching aspects I had questions with, and Dawn helped me learn how to survive in this wacky world of education. Without them, I don't know what would have happened. I highly advise any of you newbies to reach out to people like them who can keep you floating the first year. You won't regret it. Thankfully, my first class of kids turned out to be a godsend. Wonderful, fun, a bit ornery at times, but hey they were kids. I developed a bond with them quickly. I took great pride in what I taught them. I thought all is well.

This was until the principal showed up. He had offered no help in adjusting to my new home, but was quick to critique and hover to make sure I was perfect. Of course, I wasn't so we began to clash. Evaluation time came, and his example of good evaluation? "Mr. H's class was due to start at 12 and he began at 12:08." When you are bringing in 24 kids from the playground, they want the water fountain and bathrooms, so yea, I was guilty. I had not developed the skill of time management yet to the point that I could accomplish all of that and yet start at exactly 12:00. A first year teacher doesn't deserve that kind of nonsense in a matter that really isn't related to teaching skill. I had parents raving about my positive effect on their students... it didn't matter. As the year progressed I discovered that for some reason he had decided I wasn't a good fit for his building, and that was it.

To wrap this up, I began to look for jobs closer to home and with better salary. I found a position 54 miles from home, and a pay increase of $5,000. I thought I was rich! I turned in my resignation at the end of the year, and signed on for the next position. The principal with control issues decided the day I moved my stuff out he needed to come down and inspect my boxes to make sure I was taking only stuff that belonged to me... I was having visions of giving him a bloody nose, since nobody was around, and the insult of my integrity was overwhelming! Common sense prevailed, and I moved on. Before I close this chapter, I wanted to share with you a few quick tidbits-

MEMORIES OF MY FIRST YEAR ASSIGNMENT

PREPARE FOR THE UNEXPECTED

One fall day, I had the kids outside for a reading session. One of my girls, who was a timid sweetheart, was sitting nearby. As the lesson progressed, one of those "OH NO" moments occurred. A wasp had landed on her head and went into her hair. She hadn't noticed, and thankfully neither did the other kids. Not wanting a freak out session, I calmly smiled and said, "Vonna ", please sit very still okay?" She smiled and said okay. We all just sat still. Shortly, the little wasp crawled out from her hair and flew away... whew!!!

I was an assistant 7th gr. Coach for football that year. The head coach was quite a high energy loud, red faced young guy who really made no effort to include me in any phase of the coaching. I basically was a figure head. I came to find after my departure he had been fired due to "an addiction issue." I had no idea but now it makes sense.

A Success Story

I had a student in class who was the kid you remember from school who was a little big for his age. He was a little introverted and was a bit clumsy. Along the way, people had inflicted the kind of humor which would cause him to accept any deficit he had as his reality, and would result in self-deprecating humor often to get by. I established a good relationship with the kid and over time he became attached to my hip. His attendance improved, his attitude towards school got better, and most of all he seemed to feel better about himself. He is one of the success stories I look back on and feel I had a major impact in his life. I am grateful and humbled by that chance.

Stubborn Little Man

A final story of this principal that ruled his kingdom. Once it was determined I was moving on, I notified parents of what was happening and that I had enjoyed being a part of their kids' lives. The amount of thank you letters, cards, and recommendation letters that poured in were truly a comfort. The continued sentiment was their child's attitude and performance in school had greatly increased, and they were grateful for my efforts, disappointed that I was leaving the district. He was made aware of this, and he looked at me as a threat to his control in my opinion. They had no influence on changing his mind.

TRAGIC EVENT OF HISTORY IN MY FIRST YEAR AS TEACHER

An incident happened this first year of teaching that will be engrained in my brain forever. The NASA program of sending shuttles into space was going full blast. It was highly spoken of and people tuned in whenever there were updates. This year a new idea came up that grabbed the nation's attention. The idea was since space is such an integral part of study in school, why not have a contest to see if a teacher wanted to go up in the space shuttle Challenger.

We had talked this up to the students and the day came for the take-off. Keep in mind, this was before sufficient technology existed for rooms to have internet, computers, projection units, etc. We had an old TV on a library cart that we wheeled into my classroom and shared it with another class. Excitement was building as the countdown started. The kids were fixated on the action as well as the teachers. There was a segment on the female teacher who had won the contest and we were all pulling for her success.

Blast-off on a clear sky beautiful day. As the shuttle ascended a brief time, there suddenly was an enormous fireball explosion. It had blown up right before the eyes of a nation of students and teachers. There was stunned silence. Although no panic on the part of kids, the teachers knew certainly nobody could have survived that explosion. Before they had a chance to start broadcasting the reality, we decided to turn it off, explain to the kids there must have been a bad thing that happened. We will pray for the outcome, and we began to divert their attention back to learning. It is a day that you always remember where you were. I happened to be in my first classroom with no experience how to handle such a trauma with kids. I relied on my faith in God, and my instincts, and we made it thru that day. God bless Christa McAuliffe for her bravery and her ultimate sacrifice.

Fast forward eight years later, and this class reached out to me long distance and invited me to attend their graduation. For reasons I do not remember at this time, unfortunately I was unable to attend. I hope they understood. This group of kids will always have a special place in my heart.

Thankfully, this chapter of my journey was over. I had a contract for the following school year for a large urban district in the area. I knew in advance what the demographics of the district were, but after the internship in a rather big urban district, I felt I was prepared for anything. Little did I know the dramatic change that was about to come into my life.

Chapter 9

The Urban Chaos Begins

The following couple of chapters may seem a little hectic and unorganized. I hope so, because that is what this time of my journey really was to me. I hope, not only to give insight as to what the urban experience is like, but to also remember to include some brief stories, some humorous, some not, to illustrate the flavor of the environment I found myself existing as a teacher.

Time came for me to arrive at my new teaching location, in the heart of an urban district. The school system existed in a small urban city with a large population squeezed into it. Poverty, drugs, gangs, abuse, and crime was a daily existence. In this environment, their school system had one high school, one middle school, and a few elementary schools. This was a system with a large majority of African American students. As a white kid from my little backwoods town, this was as big of a cultural shock that I could have ever anticipated. I had some exposure to the urban setting and black kids in the other system, but never to this degree with this overwhelming amount of problems these kids faced on a daily basis. Let's stop here and just squelch any issues of racism on my part. I was never raised that way, and had very limited exposure to black kids in our town. I was now 27, married with one child, living 54 miles away, and now making 19,000 dollars. I was assigned the middle school, and I was going to teach 7th grade math, but when I arrived to set up my room before the school year began, I was told it would be 8th grade English. Let the fun begin!!

CHAPTER 10

THE BLACKBOARD JUNGLE

One of my favorite movies over the years oddly enough was Sydney Poitier's "The Blackboard Jungle." For many reasons, I felt I had just entered the same. As I pulled into the parking lot of the school, I realized we were not in Kansas anymore Toto. Fast forward many years to find that this building was also tore down and a new facility built to replace it. Kind of a recurring theme to have places where large chunks of your life took place no longer exists. I guess memories are something you have to be able to hold on to.

There is a certain feel to a hardcore inner city school and the neighborhood it sits in. A high rate of unemployment provides a lot of down time for folks, so you see a lot of them sitting on porches and walking the sidewalks. The homes tend to be rundown. Although not seen, there are gangs, crime, drugs, alcohol, and prostitution, around every corner. The middle school building that I was to report to was the only one in the system. It was a very old two story brick building approximately 100 yards wide at least. It had the old wood huge windows that slid open and closed top to bottom. The interior was outdated and wore down. The rooms actually had blackboards and wood floors. The halls had tile over concrete floors. This was my new educational home.

Some Very Important Career Advice

For any new teachers or soon to be teachers reading this book, let me assure you NOTHING taught in college prepares you for this kind of teaching environment. Oddly enough, many of you are idealistically looking at one of these environments as a place where you would love to work. Reason – you feel this is the student that needs you the most, and if you can reach at least one, then it will all be worth it. I commend you but also from experience advise you to think hard of your decision. When you are young, as I was when starting this part of my career, it is an ideal that is honorable. The energy it takes is part of a young person's makeup. Believe me, it will take it all. The money, we used to call it combat pay, because it was a little extra than most districts isn't enough for what you will endure.

There are varying degrees of urban environments that I taught in. This system was the first and harshest of them all. The last I taught in was a step up, but still very parallel to the original. In either case, it takes a certain skill set to survive this challenge. I saw many who had it, and did wonderful work. I saw many who did not, and tried their best to survive. Some did, and sadly many didn't.

The Reality of your Decision

It isn't every day you watch a colleague screaming at the top of her lungs to gain some control of a cafeteria table of kids, not being listened to, her screams blending in with the ungodly noise level already there. She gestured with her hands like "I am done" and walked out of the cafeteria. This is a cardinal offense, you NEVER leave students assigned to you because of the terrible things they can accomplish unattended. I watched as she walked down the hall to her room. I made sure my table was covered by another colleague next to me so I could go and check on her. You will find folks, that in our beloved profession, those who take care of you are your fellow colleagues. Honestly, it is rare you will find an administrator caring enough to help. When I reached her room, she was crying and boxing up her stuff. I said "what are you doing?" She replied "I am done, I can't do this anymore, and this is crazy." I said "are you sure?" She nodded said thanks and walked to the office to report she was quitting. I never saw her again.

The first year, maybe the first few years, you have to be a quick learner. If you think being their buddy works, it doesn't. They don't want you to be their buddy. They want structure, consistency, fairness, and expectations with consequences. I learned this from my uncle who had risen through the ranks from teacher all the way to superintendent of a system. He told me to tell the kids you don't want to be their buddy, because you see how they treat their buddies. Tell them you will be their adult friend. It worked. Over the years, this cocktail of standards proved to be very successful in management of my classroom. These skills continued to be my foundation throughout my career and very successful. Sadly, by the time my career journey came to an end, those skills had been rudely crushed and emptied, prompting my departure. Wasn't it Clint Eastwood who said in one of his movies "a man has got to know his limitations?" Truer words never spoken.

WELCOME TO REALITY

Earlier, I described the physical structure of the building. The building contained approximately one thousand 7th and 8th grade students spread into this entire structure. It was crowded. Hallways were full, and danger was always lurking. You are basically thrown into the fire in these scenarios, and wished well. The principles rarely have the time to come to rooms and check on you, they are so busy with so many other facets of their job. I think we had two assistants and one lead principle to manage this building. So, as I mentioned before, you learn to make friends with neighboring colleagues for survival. There are always good folks willing to help since they remember the day there were in your shoes. I quickly became friends with our school security guard. He was a massive black man, about 6ft. 2in., and well over 325 pounds. The man was fast as well. The kids respected him, and as we became friends, he always had my back. Over the years I would invite him, his wife, and sons to our home on the 4th of July for cookouts and fun. His friendship was valuable to me for many years. I hope he is well. You must also become friends with the school secretary, nurse, custodian, and cafeteria ladies. These folks will take care of all your needs, especially in a pinch. My teaching time here began, and the learning process quickly started sinking in for me. It is a process of feeling your way through some brand new experiences. I found quick that the students check to see if you know what you are doing, and if they can get away with anything. If you fail this part, you are doomed. Soon, I became known as a big guy that doesn't put up with any nonsense. My "rep" was established. Sure, there were still times when you were put to the test. If you keep in mind the items mentioned previously, you survive. I want to share with you one of the things these kids consider a top priority. It is you pronouncing their name right. I know you are saying, "huh?" It's true. These kids had names that I had never seen before with a lot of letters. At first, I would just pronounce what I thought it was, only to be met with "teeth smacking", "eyes rolling" and some attitude. So I learned quickly. I told them I have over 150 names each year to learn while they only had a few in the teachers they have. I would apologize upfront for any mispronunciations, and asked them to speak clearly and be patient when they correct me. I then said give me time and I will get it right. This formula seemed to work throughout my career. A little side story of humor on this topic:

Unforgettable Names

One thing you find in the urban settings is outside agencies who partner with the schools to provide speakers from their specialty to come in and share with the kids. I met one of these early on. He was a fun guy, who came to share I believe on issues of domestic violence and what they can do if they are stuck in any of it. We were talking about names one day and he said," I bet I have two that you can't possibly beat." Feeling like a bit of an expert, I said you're on! I told him a few at the time that stood out to me. We shared a few grins and he said what about this as he walked to the blackboard. He writes: lemonjello and orangejello. I was blown away. Are you kidding me? In each word, put the accent on the second syllable and you can pronounce both. Needless to say, he won.

There are several important and some humorous incidents that I would like to share with you concerning this important part of my educational journey. They follow in no particular order, just how this middle age guy remembers:

PRACTICAL EDUCATION IN THE MIDST OF CHAOS

As a newbie from a little burg, my exposure to fighting was fairly limited. I learned quickly at this middle school. First, you had to learn the current slang of the kids. The first one that surprised me was "you wanna bug?" This was an expression of a desire to fight. So, needless to say, my ears would go up when I heard kids say that remark. Then, there are times when no such remark is heard, and all chaos breaks loose. One day during class instruction I heard a female voice say, "you said what?" I turned in time to see her grab the head of the male next to her in a head lock, take her nails, and claw them down his face drawing blood. Desks flew, as this was instantly the formula for the others to go crazy. I parted the crowd as I bulled through. I grabbed the female who wouldn't stop, and had to wrap my forearm around her neck/shoulders and pull her from the room. By then, help had arrived, and I proceeded to calm the rest of them with my bellowing.

A brawl broke out in the hallway between two girls. The crowd formed around them. I approached along with the male gym teacher who grabbed the one on top. I grabbed the one on bottom. She would not stop! So, by the ankles, I had to drag her away from the scene, all the way with her swinging at nothing.

One day a prized possession of mine disappeared from my desk. I had established myself by then, so quietly I found out whom it was that had done this. I looked for him during my break and located him in a quiet part of the building. I walked up to him, pointed my finger on his chest and said "I know you have it, make sure its back after lunch, or I will come for you." I walked away. Guess what? There it was, right after lunch.

On another occasion, I was in the office area chatting with a few colleagues. As we were there, out of nowhere a student had jumped from the second floor. We were in temporary shock, stunned at what we had seen. Suddenly, this apparently nimble young man, stood up, saluted us, waved and ran away from the building. The call was made to the appropriate administrator and we went about our day as if it were just another regular occurrence.

It goes without saying; I had a huge percentage of students with incredible problems that prevented them from a normal educational experience. I found my daily routine included reminding them of their potential, encouraging them not to waste their time, and to avoid trouble so they wouldn't become another convict or worse yet, dead. I know this may sound harsh to you, but trust me, I knew these things had to be said for their own good and for my conscious to be clear that I had done my part in telling them. Here is an example of why:

We had a young girl drop over one day in an upstairs hallway. The call went out for emergency help. Our school nurse ran to the site, assessed the situation, and began CPR. Later, it was determined the girl had a heart condition and simply died. It left a heavy cloud around the school for some time. I am sure some people make it thru their whole career never experiencing the death of a student. Here I was a few years into my career, and had a few occur already. Sadly, there would be more to come later in my journey.

On the Job Experiences Continue

Later, when I was at the elementary assignment you will be reading about, I was surprised with another event left over from this middle school experience. I was walking thru the hall past an adult who I knew was waiting for his kid. As I began to walk by the guy called out to me. I stopped with a look of curiosity. He asked if I remembered him. I responded the face was familiar. He told me he was one of the group members I mentioned earlier who had one stabbed over the summer that year. I was surprised. This was a kid who gave me so much grief in trying to get him to listen and learn. Much to my surprise, it had taken hold. He told me that I always used to say that he needed to get serious about his education before it's too late. He said that he finally did, graduated school, got a job, and has a family now. I was floored. He then went on to thank me for not giving up. I told him I was glad he listened and all the headaches were worth it to find he had made something of himself. As I walked away, it was hard to conceal the big ear-to- ear grin that was filling my face.

I want to share a humorous yet oddly sad experience I had with a colleague whose friendship I enjoyed. He was an overweight guy who taught science. He had done so many years successfully. Towards the end, he went on a major diet that helped him lose a huge amount of weight. I noticed an odd peculiarity about this kind soul. When sitting around a table, engaging in conversation with him and others, he would often interrupt his words with a "sshh" that he would interject. Can you imagine? Often in his sentences, a sudden "sshh" would enter! Later, I came to find out that due to his multiple times over all his years of teaching using this to quiet his class, it had become part of his speech patterns. Poor guy. After

I was gone from this district a few years, I found that he had passed away from a heart attack in his forties. I always remember this friend. I was determined not to let that happen to me.

As I mentioned before, I was 54 miles away from this position. It took approximately 1hr.10min. to get there on a good day. We had to sign in a book in the office so the principal could see if anybody hadn't showed up that day. I actually had just signed in and turned to see another person reach for the pencil. The principal said, "I'm sorry, but you are late." What a great profession! The veteran teacher responded, "Oh, that's okay, I was coming in to let you know I am going home sick today." Touché. Another day, after school there were rumors there was going to be a major fight outside on the football field. The male teachers who were able went with the male assistant principals to see. Sure enough, it broke out. As we all did our part to send kids home, I looked to see one of the principals get punched in the face. I was in shock. I had never imagined it could happen. Although not always punches to the face, it was a scene I would see too often in the remaining years of my career that would happen to many teachers, including myself.

Administrator Variations

Before I take you to the elementary building I was assigned for the remaining years I spent in this difficult district, I want to share a bit with you on the topic of administrators. The following are a few thoughts:

> *Administrators are a necessary evil. Unfortunately, what happens is the majority forget where they came from. Sometimes, as you are in the career longer, you find many of them don't have as much experience as you have. Also, there will be some who have had very little experience but have advanced to this position due to "the inside track" of knowing somebody or being a "name" in a district. In this district I am writing*

about, I remember nine different administrators. Three of them were helpful and backed teachers in their efforts. The other six, three of them in particular, were the WORST you can imagine. I know this sounds like bitter grapes, I won't bore you with all the details supporting this observation. Honestly, some of them are caught in a bad situation. Often, they are getting pressure from unreasonable superintendents who are imposing standards that are brutal. As a result, their evaluations are based on results that teachers produce from their directive as structured by the district. The whole system then breaks down. Often, the root problem is behavior of the students. I was one of the best managers of the classroom and the student behaviors and still had a fair share of outbreaks. Teachers send them to principals hoping for progressive discipline that often would require either suspension in or out of school. The principals don't want out of school suspensions because it reflects on the attendance numbers. That, in turn, lowers the chance of the school getting the one point that urban districts count on for the state report cards so they don't come out with a zero. This ploy backfires because then teachers don't feel supported, and students realize quickly that very little is going to happen to them. Consequently, behaviors get worse, teachers become resentful, and principals are alienated.

Next, you have two schools of thought with principals. If they evaluate a teacher with all good comments that many of them deserve, they feel the teacher will become complacent and not strive to improve. The other thought is if you are a veteran teacher, you are a "dinosaur" that is resistant to change and their job is to either change you or get you so uncomfortable that they push you towards the door. Either way, this becomes not a comfortable situation. Also, be prepared for the unexpected. Here are a few I experienced-

SHOCKING ADMINISTRATOR BEHAVIOR

I was threatened by a principal in a one- on- one conversation that if I did not end my friendship with a colleague who was a union official and a friend, that my job may be in jeopardy. I was in a face to face argument with another who was angry that I had written up his nephew who was being unruly in class. One of the most arrogant, self-absorbed men I have ever met in my life, in my opinion. Imagine my shock, when from a distance, I saw him walking thru my building in the second district I worked in. He was there with a group to observe some of the accomplishments we had made at the middle school level. Needless to say, I avoided any interaction. I was evaluated by a lady who had the most ridiculous expectations for teacher performance. She was brutal. The irony is that when she tried to run a class she was run over by the students. She still maintained her goals for teachers were reasonable.

The point of this diatribe is to advise you when you find a principal who is supportive, treasure them. They are far and wide between. When you find your principal is one of those lovely people described above, protect yourself. The worst situation is when one of them puts a target on your back. Your life becomes not about teaching, but protecting your livelihood. Again, the student suffers in the long run.

Time was Running Short in this District

Life had become pretty difficult for me in the early days of my career. The drive was wearing me down, and the environment I worked in was more chaotic than you can imagine. I began looking for a way to get out. I learned something from this that is invaluable for all new educators. Here is another piece of advice:

> *If you find you are not happy in the district you are working, try to get a new position within the first 3-5 years. Districts prefer to hire people low on the salary scale, so the more experience you have the least likely you are to get a new position. This again flies in the face of common sense. One would think that experience should be a plus. In education, it often becomes a deficit.*

I was having a hard time finding districts to accept me with many years of experience. I began to look in other career choices. I found one in an opportunity to purchase a business that would get me out. It became a huge find. Around this time, the district needed to move some people. I found out I was going to be placed in the angry administrator's building who we argued over his nephew. He had taken a lead principle job at this new location. This was the final straw. I put in for a leave of absence and gambled. I made the purchase of this new business and took a year off to see if I could make it happen. The kick me sign still remained on my back unfortunately. The details follow.

Chapter 11

The Teacher Becomes a Store Owner – An Attempt at Freedom

It was the end of the 80's when video stores were booming. The one that I went to was no exception. The store had a private owner who I became friendly with and we would often go sit in his office and discuss business. It became known to me that he was preparing to sell his store. The timing I thought was perfect. It would be my way out of the blackboard jungle! We began discussing details. I did not have a business background, but on face value this seemed to be an operation that I could assume ownership of fairly easy. I had him produce the books that indicated a strong profit margin. I was able to sign for six figures and the store was mine. Before it transpired, I stood and looked this guy eye-to-eye and said, "It seems like everything is legit here, but I am telling you something, if you are lying you are messing with my family, and I won't ever forget it." He replied, "You have nothing to worry about."

I was always raised on a man's word is his honor, so given everything, it was complete. I guess not everybody was raised with that same ethic. The business never produced the income that was claimed it would produce. In addition, in the plaza where the store was located, a huge grocery chain was about to open an enormous section of their store to be a video store. It would operate as a "loss leader". This meant that they would be glad to take losses on the rental of their videos as long as while you were there you picked up a few groceries where they made their profit.

I absolutely enjoyed being an owner of a business. The freedom was invigorating. The trouble was in no time it was clear things weren't right. As a result, in a last ditch effort to be able to survive, and stay out of going back to the urban setting and the commute, I came across another business that would fit in the back of my store and partner with the current theme. It was a record store. It sold vinyl records of 45's and albums, and CD'S were just starting to develop. The store had an existing list of clients who stocked their juke boxes and disc jockeys who bought their music through this store. One would think that having been burned once already, I would not make the mistake again. I was acquainted even more with this owner who assured me it was just too much for him to handle and produced the books to see. It sure was profitable! Friends, I know you are saying "uh, oh". Unfortunately, you are correct. The whole thing was even less profitable than the store appeared.

So the addition ended up being the albatross that brought it all to an ugly end within a little more than a year run. I had just moved into a new home in the suburbs. I had been married about 10 years at that time. My son was 5, and my daughter was recently born. Now, to add to all of this, I was facing the darkness of bankruptcy. Without going into all the details, since this is mainly a book about urban education experiences, I will just say that it is one of the most humiliating experiences of my life. I have always been a gold star credit kind of guy. Fortunately, I was able to save my house, but everything else financially was now in a ruin. Oh, did I mention that my wife had just made the decision to stay home for a while to raise the kids? In hindsight, I believe this is when depression invaded my being and stayed for many years to come. Not only was I involved in all of this, I now had to face the fact I was going back to the place that had no appeal at this time. The only good thing was I had been reassigned to a different elementary building away from the angry little principal mentioned earlier. Little did I know it would end up being more of the same, even worse? The details of my days in the elementary school assignment I had in this big district will continue to fill in some blanks for you on what the urban environment offers. There is one piece of advice for those of you considering opening a business:

BUSINESS CAUTION

If you are considering a move to an owner of a business, go into it with eyes wide open. There are a lot of crooks out there, who have no honor. They will look you straight in the face and flat out lie. Investigate everything with a third party who has an objective viewpoint. If the answers aren't good, don't push it. Be able to accept no. Don't allow your desire to escape the place you are stuck in override your common sense. Things eventually work out. You have to stay focused.

Chapter 12

The Blackboard Jungle – Elementary School – How Bad Can It Really Be?

Over the next 7-8 years, my life became so busy and overwhelming; it's hard to put it all into words, although I will attempt to do so in the following section. Along with my recollection of the highlights of this assignment, (and low points), I also experienced a major surgery, a divorce, and an onset of a condition that changed my life forever. So, ultimately, the kick me sign seemed to be fixed to my back with super glue.

The average reader would think certainly my issues should get better going from the most difficult aged student recognized by all in education, to the relative peace of an elementary school grades K-6. Before I got to this point, I would have agreed with you. However, as you are about to find out, it was the same chaos, just a different age level. Here are some of the recollections I have of this assignment.

The Elementary Years in the Journey

During this time frame, I will end up working for four different administrators. Only one of them was remotely competent for the job. The rest brought personal agendas and biases to the position.

The male I worked for was a real treat. He expected any directive of his was to be followed explicitly without question. He was the one I mentioned earlier who threatened my job if I were to continue my friendship with a colleague who had a union position and who had the nerve to argue with him. His audacity knew no boundaries. One day, he stopped by the room, stood in the doorway looking around as the supreme ruler of his kingdom. This was not unusual. He was not one to compliment, he felt if you were doing your job well, that's what you were getting paid for. If you weren't, well that is when you would feel the wrath. This day I saw him scratch down something on a note, leaving it on my desk. I was excited. You see, as one of the best classroom managers of behavior, you could go up and down our hall, and my room would be on task, in their seats, behaviors in check. I thought maybe at last some recognition. I walked over, picked it up and read. It said, "You have a piece of bulletin board trim loose, fix it." Nice, huh! I was so mad I balled up the note and threw it out the door into the hallway. Probably not a good idea for you newbies, but I had been around a while and really was upset.

I also mentioned to you my hour and 10 min. commute one way. Anybody with common sense realizes that depending on traffic and weather, arrival times would vary. I made it a science to get good at it, and if I were late due to those reasons, it would only be a few minutes. I would let him know if it were my fault or one of those two things I couldn't control. This was also at a time when cell phones weren't happening yet. If I had to call so they knew I was running later than normal, I would have to find a pay phone, and make the call. That being said, one day I was making the drive following behind a semi. I watched as a car was passing him on the left and without warning he just started moving left and pushed the guy into a guardrail and an awful crash. The flow of traffic I was in glided by and then behind me started stopping and came to a halt. I noticed the truck was not stopping. My mind said if I were the guy in the car, I would hope somebody would do the right thing for me. I kept following and gesturing to the truck driver that I was writing down his plate and he should pull over and stop. Finally, he did. I then decided that being an eye witness was important to the guy in the car so that he would be taken care of properly. So I went back to the scene and waited for troopers. I made the call telling work what had happened and that I would be late. After finishing my obligation at the scene, I jumped in the car and hustled to work. My wonderful boss wasn't happy again. He said I was too late and it was not good for the kids. I reminded him that as professionals and role models for kids, we always tell them the right thing to do including civic duties and being good citizens. How could I have done anything else? He listened and said get to class. Nice, huh. Needless to say, when you were being observed by him for evaluation, your gut was in a knot, because depending on his mood, your evaluation could be fine, or you could get tore up. Fortunately, I don't recall any major issues with him when it came to my classroom performance.

A Major Nightmare

One lady I worked for was by far the most ridiculous of all four. She reminded you of a person who was so excited to have her own kingdom, she was all giddy. Her theories and her directives were supposed to be cutting edge and what was good for kids. It was a train wreck. Her expectations were out of reach. If you didn't follow them, the target was on your back, and she was gifted at making your life miserable. She had the uncanny ability to walk through the halls of chaos with a frightening smile on her face pretending that all she saw was normal for a school building. When you asked her how things were going, knowing that she had an argument with parents earlier, she would smile and say just fine. I wanted some of that magic she was displaying. Seriously, it was all phony. She was a terrible disciplinarian with kids, and believed all issues could be solved with kind discussion. It was crazy. The biggest thing I remember with her was the evaluation process. I took some lumps with her on my evaluations, with some low marks on occasion, not because I deserved it, but rather due to my inability to always be agreeing with her. At the end of one particular year, she had given me a U in a category, honestly I can't remember right now. I called our union rep, wanting to dispute it. The rep said it was in the wrong category anyway, so by rule, she would have to remove it. We had our conference and the union rep told her the information. This woman said "oh, no. we've been doing it that way for years, and that's the way it is going to stay!" My rep responded, "I wrote that part of the contract, you can't do it." The principal refused. The rep said," well, this meeting is over. We will file a grievance and over the summer it will be handled and you will lose (the principal)". School came to a close, the summer came and went all too fast, and when I returned I went to central office to check my file and see that it had been taken care of. The evaluation had disappeared. These are the realities of some of the nonsense in the big urban districts that you my friends will have to learn quickly to protect yourself.

More Leadership Fiascos

Another lady I worked for in this building was basically a curriculum leader who has been placed in this role for a short while. She was the epitome of a person who loved to hear herself speak. She enjoyed postulating about various "new" instructional techniques that more often than not weren't realistic for the environment we worked in. She would do just enough to appear involved but yet rarely get "here hands dirty." She knew she had a good gig and was only doing this for the moment, no need to get overworked or stressed. The problem was she was of very little support to the teaching staff and could not herself survive in the classroom.

The last lady I worked for in this school was probably the most qualified. She expressed herself well, and handled parental issues strongly. The only problem was she had a hint of racial overtones to her interactions, often intimating that the only teachers that can really understand "our" kids were themselves African-American. I know some of you are finding that hard to believe, but it was a theme often heard not just from her but others as well. Believe me, it caused an unusual amount of awkward moments, when as a Caucasian you were doing all you could, not seeing color of students, just students.

Almost Too Hard to Believe

An example of this type of interaction was the day we had a guest speaker in for our staff meeting. He was an African-American who had converted to Islam and arrived in a full African garment robe. Our staff was approximately 60% black, 40% white. He was there to try and illuminate the special needs that black kids have in urban settings. His opening statement, "do you know what the number one industry in America is today? The prison industry, because they want to keep brothers down." People all around were aghast, almost an audible huh could be heard. I was so angry. I simply got up, told my friend that was enough for me, and walked out. Amazingly, nothing was said.

This administrator had a better grasp on instruction than any of the previous. She just came up short in a few areas. Another problem arose when in the process of breaking up a fight between two sixth grade boys; one of them inadvertently struck me in the arm. This was the first time it had ever happened to me. Anger combined with overwhelming sadness hits you hard. I grabbed him and pushed him into the wall holding him in place and saying that's it, you hit me, it's over. When the whole mess ended up in the office for processing, her attitude came forward. I said," I need an assault form, I was hit." She calmly looked me over up and down, and said," I don't see any blood or bruises?" Through gritted teeth, I asked for the form. As I was filling it out, the parent arrived to pick up her kid. Thinking maybe I could get some support from her, I had told her I was the one who her kid had struck. Her response was "oh, okay. Where is he?" So much for thinking I might get some well-deserved support!

A final example of this principal's deficiency was an incident that occurred towards the very end of my time in this district. I had been teaching a group of sixth graders, and one I had just had to write up for behavior on recess. (Recess was an empty parking lot where you could let kids play or participate with them in kickball games.) The day ended and when I left to drive home, I noticed a lot of people on the highway pulling beside and pointing to my passenger door. Finally, I pulled over out of curiosity. Here, in big capital letters, scratched into my paint was the greeting, "F**k you." Words can't express the anger and embarrassment as I completed my drive home. School was close to over at that point. Students were released long before staff was dismissed.

The next day I went into this lady's office and asked for a vandalism form. She inquired what happened. I told her and she replied "well at least they didn't slash your tires or break your windshield." After investigating with students I trusted, it came back to me it was the student I had written up recently. When confronted, he confessed to authorities. They had promised that he would be in an offender's school in summer where he would have to work and pay back a portion of my costs to repair. I was satisfied; I didn't want him in the system. Summer came and went. When I inquired about my money, they reported he had not completed the course and no money was available to me.

Final Memories of this District and some Advice

In poorer districts, free breakfast and lunch are offered through funding available. Our district was no different. In the morning, it was frenzy, because as kids arrived, they would go to the gym, which also served as our cafeteria, for a fast breakfast. Cereal, milk, juice, sticky buns, and assorted items that didn't require any preparation were offered. My friend and I noticed an odd occasional visitor. This lady would show up in her housecoat, hair everywhere, walk in and smile, visiting along the way. She would go to the table, scoop up as much as she could carry in her arms, and head out the door, offering verbal pleasantries as she left. We would look at each other and shake our head. It was out of our reach of control, and yet nobody did anything to stop it.

Speaking of breakfast, lunch was a new experience in chaos and noise. There was a lady who was the cafeteria manager. A nice woman, but not known for her quiet side. The gym/cafeteria had four doors by which entry and exit occurred. Teachers would escort their class to the gym, drop them off since the lady had a staff, and take our own lunch thankfully in a different part of the building. The first day I did this, I was caught off guard by an earth shaking experience. This woman's method of getting the kids attention was to blow a whistle into a microphone that went over speakers in the gym! Ouch! When we would return, it looked like a tornado had hit. Papers everywhere, kids screaming, complete lunacy. Then, of course, it was the teacher's job to get them back to the room, settled down, and refocused on the afternoon lessons. Good luck with that! Of course, if there were a discipline system in place that kids realized they would be accountable to for their actions, well, I digress.

My Friend for Life

Earlier, I mentioned my friend. I had acquaintances, colleagues that you worked with and got along together, but this guy was and is a true friend that I am grateful we got to know each other. He had been in the system a few years before my arrival. We were two guys in a predominantly female environment. No offense ladies, but guys need somebody to hang out with as guys sometimes. He and I immediately hit it off. His insight and laid back demeanor was a key to my survival. I learned so much from him. We had a catchphrase that we would say to each other when things became unbearable. (Sorry, that is private) He was a talented special education teacher who dealt with some of the most difficult cases you can imagine. I owe him. We remain friends to this day.

One day, we were in the office and he was asked to go bring a 1st grade student to the office that was out of control. He asked if I wanted to help. I said sure. I could not imagine how tough it could be. When we got to the room, we found out. The boy was bonkers. We encouraged him to come to the hallway and asked him to walk with us to the office. He refused. So, we did a two man carry maneuver. Each of us took hold of one arm and carefully braced him so as to not cause hurt. We carried him this way to the office as he screamed and threw himself around. Along the way, I heard my friend say "it wouldn't be nice to bite the teacher". I looked down just as our young friend was wide mouthed and close to having a snack of my friend's forearm. Fortunately, he stopped this from happening.

We both enjoyed a female colleague for her bizarre sense of humor and her refusal to give into the system telling her what to do. She became known as a lady a little off the beaten path. She was great. Again, an example of what the system does to good people over time. She had been complaining for a while about some things in her room and things in general. Again, if you don't learn how to stay off the principal's radar, you can make life miserable for yourself. At the end of this particular year, she was informed she was being moved to a small classroom with younger kids right next door to the music room. This put her over the edge. Clearly, it was a deliberate payback for her complaining, but she couldn't do anything about it. Another guy who had been complaining was told he was going from 1st grade, which he taught his entire career, to 6th grade which he had never done. He begged for relief. None was offered. Over the summer, he had a nervous breakdown and filed/retired on disability. This career can be brutal. At any rate, our female friend was in her last year, so she decided she had to maintain her dignity. Instead of it getting the best of her, she zoned out. One day I came to her room to say hi, when I opened the door, it was a circus. Kids everywhere, noise deafening. I said are you okay? She looked up and said well they don't want to help me, and I can't teach over the music noise, so I gave them some work and I am balancing my checkbook! I was stunned, but proud of her defiance which gave her some dignity. As we spoke, a student who had been on the carpeted floor started a slithering movement towards the door. I gestured to her and she said, "Oh let him go he comes back!" I hope she is okay today. Somehow, she probably is just fine.

Self-Preservation Advice

I share these things because one of the critical issues you readers need to get established is that of self-preservation. We all get into this field thinking that we can teach children effectively and we will do what we need to reach them. This is certainly an idealistic, honorable intent. The truth is if you find yourself in an urban environment, it is both rewarding and draining. The younger you are the more durability you have in dealing with the rigors specific to this kind of environment. Be warned, people in urban education, especially administration and those teachers who have reached the point where they aren't able to change their environment, will tell you there is no difference between urban and suburban education environments. With all due respect, this is nonsense.

In addition, there are more changes and demands placed on you than suburban educators due to poor test scores. Some right now think how did he know about my district? It is a common deficiency that our system tends to blame teachers for. As this thing progresses, more systems will start to tie their salary schedule to test scores. Frequently, in an attempt to show accountability to the public, districts will bring in the newest program at any cost. It's ironic how there is never money for raises, but always money for new programs. They all promise successful improvements in scores. What they fail to acknowledge, and the districts will never say this, is that unless parents do their part and students buy into the improvement hopes, these new programs are doomed to fail. A lot of people right now are saying oh he must have been resistant to change! No, experience shows you quickly what will and won't work in the classroom.

However, districts want the veterans to move into retirement, because they feel they can manipulate the newbies more easily.

Don't let them do that! Self-preservation will prolong your career. Do what is right for you in the classroom and out, while doing what you feel is right for your students. Draw a line in the sand, and don't cross it. Learn how to do as much as you can at work, and don't let it invade your home life. Enjoy yourself away from work as well. Take care of you before anyone or anything else, trust me, nobody else will.

The Good and the Bad

A quick digression for a moment. One of the worst examples of manipulating the system is a guy I worked with at the middle school in this district. I found myself always pushing to get sufficient grades in the book to adequately evaluate student performance. There were always pressing deadlines that I was up against. Although I never missed a deadline, the tension was difficult. One day I went next door to inquire how he managed the same issue. I walked up to him to find him with his gradebook open to pages with a roster of names and no grades. When asked about this subject, he calmly with a smile said "This is how I deal with it." He then took a pencil and filled in both pages with grades out of thin air. He also made sure only a few failed for that grading period in order to keep administration off his back. Imagine my shock! Although I never did that, I kept in mind not to let it get the best of me.

Every now and then in your career, you will find somebody who epitomizes the professional educator. There was a lady in this building who I will never forget. She was married, with a couple older kids, and had been teaching for some time. She was outstanding. She had a great relationship with the students, and a good outlook on our environment which I was envious of. She gave of herself way and above what was expected. Many nights in the classroom, many hours of work at home. At times, she would have to miss some family activities, but always felt the need to reach higher for the students. Many would say that is what you are supposed to do! True, but not at the sacrifice of yourself or family.

This lady was in her forties, when she suddenly passed away. I remember sitting at her funeral listening to her two young men speak fondly of their mom and see the husband tore apart. With all due respect to her and her memory, I vowed that day to never forget that in the end this is a job! It is a career, a high calling. If you don't keep things in priority, it will swallow you up and it will be too late.

A Potential Disaster Averted

Before I forget, another student event that will never be forgotten and a lesson you can learn from. One of the most irritating things you will discover in the upper middle school grades is the desire for students to run to the bathroom multiple times per day. If you don't take kids as a group, you have to establish rules for restroom use that work for you. That aside, one day one of my big boys who was known to be a joker, started with his hand up multiple times for this purpose. He knew our rules, and I spoke out that they needed to be followed. In a short while, I saw this was a necessary trip. I excused him. He hustled down to the restroom and was gone for some time. I sent another boy to check on him. He told me the original boy had an accident and had sent for the custodian. Certainly, not news a teacher wants to hear. As I was in the hall outside my door, here the student comes, grinning ear to ear. As he was nearing, the odor preceded him! At the same time, the custodian stepped out from the bathroom and yelled, "Hey, get back here, I'm not cleaning that up!" It turns out, my joker student had decided a great way to get out of school was to drop his pants and spray physical waste around the stall walls. In addition, he also felt it would be funny to use his fingers to "paint" in the mess. When the parent came up to pick joker up, she began questioning why I didn't let him go to the bathroom, which obviously was not the case. I said, "I think I would worry more about getting him home and cleaned up before other students catch on to what is going on." Thankfully, she agreed. The moral of the story? Beware of the bathroom!

LIFE'S OTHER SURPRISES

Away from the classroom, there were three life - changing events in addition to the bankruptcy previously mentioned that occurred which further depleted my physical, mental, and emotional health. Each of these three was in themselves enough to destroy an average person. By the grace of God, I managed to survive. Although the effects were long lasting, I pushed on, desperately trying to take the kick me sign off my back. The following section gives you some insight to each of these events and what occurred:

SURGERY

Over a period of many years, I had been developing a thyroid goiter in my neck. My doctor had been monitoring it, treating it with thyroid supplement. As it continued to grow, our efforts to stunt its growth had failed. A biopsy determined it was not cancer, thank God. My morbid fear of surgery and never waking up from the anesthesia caused me to postpone the inevitable many years. It continued to grow. I would wear shirts with high collars to try and hide it. It became impossible and quite unsightly to view. One day as I walked into a store, as a kid was coming out, he said, "Oh, what's wrong with your neck?" This incident was followed by my doctor taking a complex x-ray to find that I had a 1 cm. opening left in my airway. It had also been causing some heart rhythm problems, as well as breathing issues. The time had come to face the knife. I was referred to a specialist with the local hospital. He was known for his surgical skills in this area. It turned out to be a good thing because his skills were about to be tested to his limits. Upon examination he stated he had seen worse and that this would be about a 2hr. surgery followed by a 1 hr. recovery period. The time came for the fear to be faced. I asked God to be with me during this time, and to make sure I woke up okay. I had two young kids by then, and they needed their Dad. Thankfully, my prayers were answered. The pre - surgery routine was a bit tense with some of the preparations needed. I then heard, "Okay, we are going to put you to sleep now…" as instantly I went black. It ended up being a 4 ½ hr. surgery and a 2 ½ hr. recovery. It turned out the thyroid had wrapped itself around the trachea and attached itself with many appendages to the wall of the interior neck. He had to carefully expose each attachment, cut it, and move to the next. All along the way, there had to be careful deliberate cuts to not cause paralysis of vocal cords or facial nerves not to mention the many blood vessels in the area. The doctor earned his pay that day for sure. It was a very foggy, very long process of recovery that day in my room that extended well into the night, and even part of the next day. It was traumatic waking up to see the results as well as feel the pain. It felt as if my head would fall off my neck if I were to move. The next day at noon they asked if I wanted to go home. Can you imagine? The surgeon was outstanding, but the aftercare left a little to be desired. I believe they were understaffed. At any rate, the following day I went home and began what turned out to be a six week period of recovery at home.

DIVORCE

When I had been in the field for about 10 years, my life took an abrupt change. I know some of you are thinking what else could it be? Remember, that kick me sign was still super glued on my back and it was paying dividends. My wife informed me she wanted a divorce. It took me down hard. I had a 10 and 6 year old at the time, I was neck deep in trying to survive in my career, and we had bought a nice new home about 5 years earlier. I liken divorce to experiencing a death. As time passed, we attempted to fix it and we found it wasn't happening. The focus next became the best way to take care of the kids. I was not interested in being a part time dad, and I knew my income as a teacher would not be able to provide for them well, and allow me a decent income for my own life. Fortunately, although I was bitter towards my wife, she understood as well, so we proceeded to iron out an agreement that was in the best interests of the kids. Basically, it was a shared parenting agreement in which they lived at both places, with them staying with me a little more than her. We covered expenses in a shared manner. The judge who heard our final dissolution said that he had never seen a case where the parents did such a good job of taking care of the kid's needs. During the initial year or two, I had to be strong for my kids. I never left when they were with me. If I had to answer some tough questions as I tucked them in at night and wiped away their tears, I would go downstairs in the dark, squeeze my head in frustration, and cried quietly for God to help me in this hour of need. Thankfully, he was there every time. I never bad mouthed the kids' mom, and always tried to accommodate her needs since she was cooperative in the kid's best interests. This is the key folks because the kids still love both parents equally. If I were to have verbally destroyed their mom, not only would it damage the kids, but they would forever resent me for it. My parents lived nearby and thankfully my mom was available to help with the kids. It was a godsend. I am satisfied that they ended up as well as they could have given all circumstances. Did they suffer any damage? Sure, there has been some, it's impossible for there not to be. However, both have graduated college, married, and are gainfully employed. They live an hour or so away from me, and we are always in touch. They keep this middle age guy happy to be the best dad I could be. So, even though this was a major kick from the kick me sign, I was staggered but continued to push on.

Atrial Fibrillation –
The Day I Thought I Was Going to Die

As I recall, it was a Friday and I was in the middle of my commute home from work. It had been the normal chaotic week, nothing out of the ordinary. I was tired, and had things on my mind. As I was driving, suddenly my heart began a chaotic racing pulse rate. It would not stop, it got worse. I am not talking mildly. The best description is if you have been fishing and had a fish on the hook, the thrashing wiggle that you feel as you bring it in, was now my heart in my chest. Breath was rapid. There was no pain, just a sense of weakness from this onset. To be honest, I thought this must be some kind of heart attack. I was scared. I couldn't take it anymore, so I pulled into the parking lot of a small business. As I got out of my van, I fell to the ground, confused, scared, and praying. The owner came out and asked what's wrong. I told him I thought I was having a heart attack, call 911. He came back after he called and I told him "If I don't make it, tell my wife and kids how much I love them." He told me to hang in there help is on the way. I am thankful for his help.

Rather than get into all the details of what occurred over the next few days, I will tell you it ended up being atrial fibrillation. I was in my mid-thirties. This wasn't supposed to happen. One of the most annoying things paramedics and docs do during their attempts at treating you is tell you to calm down. It's just crazy they say that! You have no control over your heart rate. It is racing anywhere between 160 and higher, and doing so erratically. All you want is do something to slow my heart rate down. This was the first in a series of emergency room visits to find out how to fix this over the next several years. It was brutally frustrating. It would often happen in the middle of the night and you would wake up to the feeling, knowing what you had to do. They admit you to the cardiac ward, where you are with mostly men of much older age. The fear, anxiety, and depression that flood your soul is numbing. Finally, through the skill of my cardiologist, he found a combination of pills that would manage the heart rate when it would slip into fibrillation rather than normal sinus rhythm. I was told if the rate stayed under 100, I could live with it. The episodes would occur and I learned to trust God, and the medicine, to get me through it. Fast forward many years, it eventually slipped into chronic atrial fibrillation where it stays. My rate is manageable, and when the ablation procedures are fine tuned to guarantee atrial fib patients success, I will consider the procedure rather than take pills forever. As I look back, the kick me sign gave me a big boot through these years, but I am still standing, and although it settled down, the sign was holding on.

At this point of the journey, it is approaching the late 90's and I am desperate to escape this environment I find myself entrenched in. My two cousins had been teaching in an urban school district back home for many years, and always said they thought I would do fine working there. There was a saying, if you can teach where I was at the time, you can teach anywhere. Experience and salary always seemed to be the stumbling block. One day my cousin said they are hiring and I can get you an appointment with my principal, who if you get past her, she will recommend you to personnel for an interview. Trying not to get my hopes up, I told her absolutely, let's do that. She went and made the appointment. This date and interview would prove to open the door to the second half of my urban educator career. The experiences, good and bad, I had no idea what they were. We now move to the interview that changed the direction of my journey. Please, read on.

Chapter 13

Interview with My Next District Assignment – Coming Home

I arrived for my interview appointment with my cousin's principal of her elementary building. The principals would interview and then recommend or not the candidate to personnel for an interview. At the completion of this interview, the lady said, "I don't know why you haven't been working for our district already. I will put you in touch with personnel right away." Within a few days, I had my appointment and interview downtown. The personnel lady hired me on the spot. I was amazed that they gave me a salary start in which I only lost 4 years of experience on the scale. It still was a loss, but not a severe one. The time on the road along with the stress of that first district was enough to justify the move. I accepted.

She then told me my position would be in the middle school. I wasn't real thrilled to go back to that age child, but experience was calling. The building also housed 5th graders and that was my first assignment. The day I arrived, my lead principal for that building came out from his office to greet me. It was still summer, and he was there cleaning as I was there to set up the room. He worked with two assistant principals, a male and a female. I will tell you now these were the three best people I ever worked for in my career without question. His hair was all ruffled; ill-fitting shorts on and muscle tee-shirt as well. He walked me to my room assignment where his introduction was, "you've been hired to teach, if any of these kids gives you any crap, send them to me and I will take care of it." My grin could not be contained. Finally, an administrator who supports teachers! I was thrilled. I began to set up shop and look forward to a new beginning. On top of it, I was 20 min. from home!

The first few years were spent in 5th grade working with a great staff of 5th grade teachers. There was a great camaraderie that I remember fondly to this day. Combine that with a positive influence of these administrators, and things definitely were upgraded with this new assignment. This building was massive, three stories and spread out over a large parcel of land. At one point, we had over a thousand students in 5-8th grade housed here.

This first assignment was where I took a gun off of a student. Some students had come to me and reported this kid who had been showing it earlier in the day. Of course, even though this kid was always in trouble, he and I had a good relationship. I took him privately in the hall and said "I know you have it, where is it?" He walked with me to his locker, opened it, and pointed to the bottom. I reached in and pulled out what I thought was a major chrome plated handgun. I quickly wrapped it in his jacket and tucked it under my arm. I told him I couldn't make this go away. He understood. I took what turned out to be an air pellet gun to the office. They called school security and the retired policeman came to retrieve it. The kid was suspended and expelled for the remainder of the semester. The officer was livid that I took it upon myself to retrieve the gun. I explained, where I had taught before, this was just another day.

This was still a hardcore inner school environment, but somehow the kids here had just a little softer edge. I spent the first few years getting to know the district's expectations, how our school operated, and the subject matter of what I was teaching. All along the way, I was developing a reputation of a no-nonsense kind of guy, but yet one that the kids enjoyed being around. My uncle, who was a superintendent in Michigan, told me early in my career, "You don't want to be their buddy, because you can see how they treat their buddies. You want to be their adult friend." Kids expect and need structure. My personal opinion is part of our current educational downfall is this idea that we need to allow kids a free environment, group work, independent of the teacher. While some of that is okay, having that exclusive of teacher directed learning does the kids no favors. I mentored a new teacher whose biggest downfall was he tried to be their funny pal. The result was total classroom chaos. Then, when he tried to get control, there was no respect because he was their funny pal.

I was also developing a reputation with the administrators as a guy who had been thru the fire and could be of help to newer teachers and those new to the urban, middle school environment. One of these administrators was a lady who turned out to be the best administrator I ever had the pleasure of working for. We developed a strong collegial relationship which proved helpful. The next few years were spent on the other side of the building with her as my lead principal. They were the best years of my career. The other side of the building had been remodeled and set up to contain 5th grade classrooms, leaving 6-8th on the original side. Soon, we packed up and migrated to the other side. The fifth grade wing was born and it is where I spent the next few years.

Chapter 14

Fifth Grade Wing – Good Times, Good Memories

They had done a great job of remodeling this wing and converting it for a fifth grade wing. I was thrilled with my new room and soon set up shop ready for the new school year. The first or second year I was there, my reputation as a strong classroom manager had preceded me. One day, a knock at the door revealed the unit principal who had come to inform me of a change. One thing new teachers will learn is when an administrator isn't asking you to do something, it generally is expected you will do what they are asking. She proceeded to say that a male student would be joining me. I asked for a while or permanently. She responded permanently. It turns out his reputation was well known. He was muscular for his age, and borderline behavior issues were a daily event. She felt he would do well with me, given my reputation and being a male.

He had been driving his female teacher to the point of a breakdown, so he came aboard. I had learned how to have private conversations in hallways with students where I was able to convey the way it was going to be. He could see he was no longer the boss. To top it off, he had no male presence in his life, so he quickly enjoyed our chats of sports. One day, when they had changed classes, one of the students was sent to get me quickly. It turns out he had faked an injury of his leg by bumping a desk, and falling to the floor, yelping and making a scene, refusing to get up. I threw the door open, barked his name, told him get quiet, get up, and get out of this room. Immediately he came bounding out with a silly grin on his face. I proceeded to remind him that he just embarrassed me by doing that with another teacher. He apologized and we never had any major issues thereafter. I often think of him and wonder where he is now. I hope he is okay.

Odd Behaviors

There are times in urban education where you will feel like Al Pacino's character did in "Justice for All." At the end, where he was sitting on the court steps basically wondering what nuthouse he was in, and his buddy lawyer walks by, tips his toupee, and says good morning. That look Al had I think was on my face on a few occasions in my career. One day, I was walking down the hall as the school psychologist was walking a student back to class. Suddenly, the student jumped on the coke machine and started climbing up the side. The look was on my face. I would have barked for him to get off the machine NOW. The psychologist said in a calm voice for him to get off the machine. The psychologist said he is to be allowed to de-escalate. HUH? I was stunned. The same student on entering the building one morning came running up the steps screaming at another kid. I shouted "Hey!" He was amazed anybody had yelled at him. He said, "Who is you?" I said, "Who is me, no, who is you?" He didn't know what to say or do, and I told him get quiet and get to class which he did.

Also, it was at this time and location where I found a disturbing incident that out of necessity we tried to create some humor. Apparently, a female student had gone into the bathroom and left a "present" on the floor of the bathroom. Can you imagine the shock? Later, we referred to the incident as the "Phantom pooper."

In these environments, you will find a lot of students who are on SSI. Others, whose parents are looking to get them on SSI. For those who are legitimate, I have no problem helping that effort. One day, I was told a student in my class was an "elective mute." I know you are wondering what that is, because I did too. He would decide when he would speak or not speak! I said, "No, that's just a kid being a brat and throwing a tantrum." For the remainder of the year, I treated him like all students. He never had an issue. One time, he got a mischievous look on his face as if he were going to not answer. I calmly looked at him and told him I had asked him a question and I expected an answer. After a pause, he responded. Elective mute issue resolved.

I was fortunate during the time I spent in the fifth grade wing to have worked with several great colleagues, gifted at their craft, which we became a major support system for each other. Believe me; you need to have your colleague friends to get you thru sometimes. We would say we needed some "Porch time". This was an area outside the one friend's room and we pulled up a few chairs in the morning to prepare for the day. Part of that, was telling stories, and letting off steam. Those were some great times.

Colleagues, Friends, Support System Stories

I would like to take a moment and share a few things about those colleagues, my porch friends. The other gentleman in the group was a gifted veteran teacher. We developed a friendship quickly. As time passed, I could see that the environment was starting to swallow him up. He could retire based on years, but chose to keep going. His wife was also a teacher in the district. He started to have various physical problems. One day, a kid came over and said he was sick. I ran next door to find him on the floor hugging the garbage can vomiting. I got the kids to my room and called for the nurse. She came up and checked him, then sent him home. Another day, we were coming in from the parking lot after a fire drill. We had just begun to go upstairs when somebody mentioned he was down in the parking lot. I grabbed somebody to watch my kids and ran out to see if he was okay. People had gotten to him by then and were sending for help. I came up to check on him. It turns out he had fainted. My worries grew larger. I kept encouraging him and his wife to take the severance offer and get out while he could still enjoy his life. He would waiver. Finally, he took the offer and left. A few years later I ran into him at the local store. He had always been a friendly type who loved a good conversation. He seemed really tired and quiet to me. It broke my heart. After we said our goodbyes, I swore that would never be me. I never realized how close it would get.

My actual teaching partner was another porch friend. She had come to our building under a cloud because the elementary building she was in had a tough female principal who didn't care for her. She transferred to our building rather than risk further conflict. She was fragile from the experience, but I encouraged her to have a fresh start which she did. This young lady went on to be an assistant principal in our building. Later, she was the lead principal in another elementary building. Finally, she was a lead principal in the last building I worked in. Did I mention the tough lady ended up being the assistant superintendent of the district? She was also the lady who had recommended me for hire. Go figure.

A young guy with a great personality and vitality for the job was part of us as well. He was one of those you knew could handle anything that came his way. He had been there a year or two, when he came to me for advice. He had an opportunity to move to a rural school and coach basketball as well. He asked if I thought he should. I told him if he didn't I would grab a two-by-four and smack him. He understood. He took the job and for years came by to thank me for the advice. He said it was the best thing he could have done. He remains there today as happy as you can be in this career.

I hesitate to mention the last lady. She was always my closest friend in teaching from the 2nd year I was in the district. A very good teacher, married, with two daughters. She attended my wedding, and both my kids graduations, and I believe their weddings. We attended one of her daughter's graduations. So suffice it to say, we were close and depended on each other for survival. This is where it gets tough. Later, when it all came to an end for me, I had texted her something and never heard back. Just complete quiet. I let it go for a while, and tried a few months later. She answered, apologized, said that she was offended over something she had taken the wrong way, and felt that since I no longer was working that we had no common ground to relate to. I was baffled. I reminded her of the above items, and tried to maintain texting. It soon fizzled out again. As of this writing, it hasn't returned. This has been a tough one for me since she was one of the few that I counted as a friend. She still works in the district. She is an outstanding teacher, and a person I still value as a friend. One day, I hope it can be restored. The loss of the day- to- day conversation with her left me with an empty spot. I wish her all the best and I hope someday, sooner than later, our regular friendship is restored.

One day I stepped into the boys' restroom to get a paper towel, and found the colleague that I mentored backed into a corner, basically talking to himself, and having a breakdown. It was scary. I asked him hey bud what's going on? He kept repeating, "I can't do this, I can't do this." I put my hand on his shoulder and said, look at me. He did and I said "You can do this. We dispense information, those who are here to get it, will. Those who don't try to get it won't. Simple as that." After a few other words of encouragement, a focus came into his eyes. He told me thanks and said he was okay. I walked him down to the dean of student's office so they could chat with him and see if he needed any relief. From that point on, he maintained I saved him that day, and would always call me Godfather. His biggest downfall was he tried to be the students' buddy, which caused him to lose control of his class when it was time to get serious.

Later on, he went thru a messy divorce, and went on a crash diet. It wasn't good. He would survive on those energy drinks that I warned him about. Years passed, and I heard he had suffered a stroke. He was in his early 30's. He almost died. The result was paralysis and a loss of verbal ability. I visited him in the hospital, and it broke my heart. He knew who I was, and tried to speak, but couldn't and became agitated. He is alive today, to my knowledge in a rehabilitation home. I often wonder if I did him any favors by "saving him" that day.

I want to take a moment here and mention a guy who was a friend and a good principal. He worked in this building during this time. Always a jokester, you could count on him for a smile and a laugh. He tried to make our lives as educators a little easier. He attended my wedding and danced with my angel principal, which is on our wedding DVD. Sadly, he retired at age 57 and three years later, died. He was playing racquetball and took a break. As he sat at the table, he simply slumped over and died. I never forgot that, and again, promised to never let that be me. I miss him.

CHAPTER 15

ONE OF THE RARE GREAT ONES

Earlier in the book, I mentioned several administrators, most of which came up woefully short in being competent. There is one who rises to the top of all leaders for which I worked. The lady was a bright, experienced, articulate lady who had the rare combination of also being a people person. She supported her teachers, and we knew it. We also knew if we messed up, she would take us aside privately, and humanely encourage you while firmly stating that this must change. You never felt demeaned or spoken down to. Her energy was contagious. In the face of the worst circumstances, she remained positive and supportive. She had a complete dedication to our students, and they knew it as well. She built morale in the building, and all of us wanted to come to work each day. For the time she was there, it was the best years of my career. I will speak later about her departure, and return to a different position, also unfortunately her un-ceremonial dismissal at the end. Remember, appreciate the good ones, they are far and wide between.

Chapter 16

9/11 Terror and the Darkness

It was Sept. 2001, the beginning of a new school year. I was teaching 5th grade in the new 5th grade wing. It was school picture day; a beautiful, sunny, blue skies Tuesday morning. My class had been called to the auditorium for their turn.

As the kids were progressing thru the line getting their picture taken, my favorite principal who I mentioned above came over to me. She asked if I had heard what happened in NYC. I told her I had not. She continued to tell me a plane had hit the World Trade Center tower. She knew my brother lived in Manhattan, and worked in the city so of course she was trying to be considerate of my potential panic. I had been there of course and I knew the size of these massive structures. I envisioned some little Cessna aircraft accidently hitting one. She walked away and in a few minutes came back and said "I will watch your class, go to the nurse's office and watch the TV."

At this point, an ice ball formed in my stomach, something was wrong. I jogged to her office to watch the TV which was already on. I was as shocked and terrified as we all were that dreadful day. By now, the first jet had hit the tower, and replay clips were being shown, with announcers speculating on what could have happened. Nobody knew. As I was focused on the TV, the second plane came in live behind the second tower striking it and igniting a fireball that resembled a nuclear blast cloud. You could hear a collective gasp go up from the announcers, and people watching. It was clear, this was no accident. Stories started coming in about a plane that had turned around over northeast Ohio, western Pennsylvania and was on course they thought to the White House. The passengers on that plane ended up overpowering the hijackers. Unfortunately, the terrorists flew the plane directly into the ground where all perished in a field in Pennsylvania. Then, the news came in that the Pentagon had been hit. Next, you see the President being notified as he was reading to some kids at a school. Our precious country was under attack by terrorists. All I could think of, where is my brother?

I grabbed my cell phone and dialed. The unthinkable came over the earpiece. The call could not go thru. The Big Apple was almost cut off. Was he doing business in the towers? Was he on the street when the buildings came down?? Where are my brother and his wife who also works in the city and was pregnant with my first nephew? A few tries later, and I managed to get thru to the secretary. I asked her where he was located. She said he came in, told his employees they needed to decide what is best to do for them and their families, but he was going to find his wife. Remember friends, at this point, all transportations were silenced in the city. He was on foot, it turned out for a couple mile jog to his wife's place of work, where he found her and headed home on foot.

All day came and went with no ability to get thru to him. It was actual torment. Parents were coming to pick up their kids early. As soon as I was able to leave, I went to where my kids were at their mom's house. I sat them down, we watched replays, and I explained to them what was happening. I told them we are okay; our country will take care of this. They seemed to be fine, youth is a wonderful thing. Finally, about 7 in the evening, my little brother calls. I yelled at him for making us crazy, but in truth, overwhelmed by the fact he was okay. He said the air smells like an electrical fire. He said they are home and safe, but nobody can come or go. I told him stay home; we loved him, stay safe. Later that night, I found out that I had not escaped this horrific incident unscathed. My brother called late. He had been drinking, and proceeded to tell me Matty is dead. A good friend of his and a friend to me, Matty, was in the second tower on the 98th floor. He never made it out. I think of him often and hope that his passing was quick. Matt was a good guy, 36 years old. God bless you friend, you are missed.

PEOPLE SKILLS OF MY FAVORITE ADMINISTRATOR

There was another time that stands out in my mind where this lady went above and beyond for me. We had an intervention/discipline room where we sent kids who had been warned but continued to disrupt class. I did this with a student. The student came back really quickly, which went against the policy of them setting in the room for one period. I wrote a short note explaining my perspective and sent the student back. The student returned again with a note. The assistant principal who was monitoring the room at the time had written the note.

REALITY

You will find in the larger districts, often urban, that a whole lot of politics, sleeping around, a group that is on the inside and picks who gets in, are common place. Sometimes, you will find it impossible to advance, and you will find many incompetent people who supposedly know more than you and are better at doing what you do, in charge of you. When this happens, stay off their radar, do all you can for students, and look to get out of the district if you can.

Now, back to the details of the note he had sent up with the kid. It was a rude one that said I must have a lot of time on my hands to be writing him notes on kids. I was furious. I asked my next door teacher friend to keep an eye on the room because I was set to tell him nose- to- nose what I thought of his note. As I opened my door, this angel of a lady had heard what he wrote in the note and sprinted across the building, knowing that if I got it, there was going to be a blow up. She stopped me and said she knows what's in the note and please stay up here. He will be seeing you later to apologize. I told her only for you would I agree to do that. Later, he did come up and shake my hand offering an apology, and I accepted, letting him know if it wasn't for her, I was on my way down to see him and I wasn't happy. He understood, and we let it go.

I thought hopefully my days of difficult administrators were behind me. Little did I know what was right around the corner. Somewhere in this few year time period, my tremendous favorite administrator made the decision to leave the district for a great job in the suburbs. During the picnic to say goodbye, the staff was in tears as well as she. Humble, thankful to know us, proud of us, she printed a letter to us that I still have today. A class lady top to bottom that would go to the mat for any of "her" teachers. Later, our paths would cross again. But, for now, the kick me sign gets real big and a bull's-eye is placed on it as well.

Chapter 17

Finally, a Chance to Be Creative

It was the end of the school year, and assignments are given out. One thing in inner school districts is if you are in the clique, you are taken care of with assignment preference. If not, you are in the luck of the draw. Well, we were approaching the 2005 school year and I was told I was being moved to 7th grade math, which of course I never had taught. Makes sense huh. About a week before school opened, I went up to move my room to the new location. I was approached by the new principal who informed me I could take the health class if I wanted it.

Reality – Choose your License well

A quick word on this subject assignment to consider. I was working with a 1-8 elementary education degree/license. This meant any subject in these grades was fair game. The inner school uses this to their advantage and moves you at will like a chess piece to fill empty classrooms. This is due to a large turnover rate year- to-year for obvious reasons. Generally, you end up migrating towards subjects you are strong in when given that chance. In suburban/ rural districts, teachers are allowed to remain in the same subject/ grade level for the majority of their career, with the appropriate belief it allows teachers to gain expertise in a certain area, which of course benefits students. In urban districts, the common belief is that if you allow a teacher to become comfortable then they become complacent. Also, the common knowledge that they can move you at any time is a control factor that they enjoy. Not to mention, if you think your union will intervene, you are sadly mistaken as I was. The majority of union negotiated contracts have loopholes in them that management uses frequently. It is extremely frustrating. Now, the licensing is far more subject- specific so this isn't too often an issue except for those who are on the old licenses as I was.

After a second to pause from the shock, I happily said that would be fine. I was now the new health teacher. A little background to what this meant. Health was a forgotten subject in our district. It was a rotation class that kids were assigned for a grading period like music, art, and gym. The guy who had been in the class and had just retired after 30 plus years was a gym teacher who also taught health. God love him, he had no materials unless he provided them. He had no direction. He did what he thought he could do and the years passed by. Some would say it was his fault, but I would say it was the failure of the system to recognize the importance of this rotation class and provide it with the proper materials while giving it the attention it deserved. A new course direction was about to begin, the man with the kick me sign had a chance to be creative and teach. Yea baby!

Chapter 18
Health Class

Before I get to one of the more enjoyable periods of my career, please allow another small digression to illustrate the mindset this new principal, former friend of the angel principal who had now left, was about to display. This was a shocker:

It was the first official day of her new leadership which is set aside for staff meetings and opening preparation. We all had a taste of what she was like by the year or two she spent as an assistant under her friend's leadership. We assembled in the library to get ready for the meeting. As we all settled in, the doors opened to a large box being wheeled in on a cart. We looked around wondering where she was and what was this box? Suddenly, she pops out of this thing! We were stunned. She was wearing a toga and bare feet. She hopped up on the library counter to sit, crossed her legs, and started jiggling her bare foot, when she proclaims: "IT'S A NEW BEGINNING, AND TIME TO START THINKING OUT OF THE BOX!" To those of us, which were the majority, who loved our former leader, this was an ultimate insult to her. How about that for appreciation?

After I moved my stuff to the health class room, I began to sense the enormity of my assignment. As mentioned, there was nothing for me to start. I investigated and found out some basic concepts that should be covered in the 6-8th grade years in health. I then went out and began to purchase what I could get my hands on. I then sat down and began to build a half dozen basic units that covered the concepts mentioned before.

It started as a hybrid type of instructional unit. My feeling initially was they only would have me for six weeks in each grade level, so each year we would modify a bit but basically continued to reinforce that which had been taught before. Remember, the kids knew the reputation of this class for many years was show up and do a couple things and basically you got your grade. This was all quickly changing. The nice part was they began to adapt well to the new material. THEY WERE INTERESTED! This is the thing all educators are excited by, student involvement in the material. My creative juices were flowing. I also had added a couple units on drug and alcohol use, as well as tobacco. These were the most exciting of all. The interest was off the charts. This subject had oddly rarely been mentioned in any previous classes, and the kids were hungry for knowledge and had plenty of questions. It was exciting.

Soon, the reputation began to spread and people became interested in what was going on. One of my greatest compliments ever received was when the curriculum department came by. They said they had heard some good things and wondered if they could look over what I had put together. I told them feel free to browse. They were impressed, and asked if I would be willing to share this with the other health teachers in the district. See, there really wasn't anything prepared or offered anybody, so everybody did what they thought was right. Sad, when you think about it. A subject as critical as this topic put on the back burner and no attention paid to it. By the way, in the four years I was in that position, the new principal never once visited my class, even after I had invited her to stop by several times. There was no interest in me or what I was doing. Once again, somehow the kick me sign glowed on my back.

After four years of excited instruction time, it came to a halt as suddenly as it started. Some higher up who had long been removed from the classroom, had decided that with the changes going on in the district in terms of shutting buildings, relabeling sections, building new buildings, it was time to let health be part of the P.E. instructional time. This of course, is a disaster. First, gym teachers like to be in the gym with students. When kids go to gym, they expect to be physical in the gym. Upon finding part of this excited time was now going to be classroom learning time, they shut down their interest. I begged to not let this happen, because our kids needed the info. There is so much marijuana usage at such an early age with our kids, along with alcohol, and domestic violence that it would be a disservice to them. Of course, not being part of the power clique, nobody listened. They shut me down, and told me I would be moving.

Now, the principal, who by now apparently decided she wasn't a fan of mine, initially told me I was going to move to the third grade and teach all subjects. My knees buckled. I had never taught below fifth except for one year when I started. The rest of the time, I was your "standard" middle school teacher. I had nothing for the little ones, although my general license seemed to think I should be prepared. I assure you folks K-3 is a very specialized area that requires tremendous nurturing people to do the job. I immediately began investigating any options I might have. The curriculum people came by and asked if they could have my material to give to the other gym teachers who were now teaching a little health. There was no way I was going to GIVE all my hard earned work and material purchased out of pocket and let others claim credit for the outcome. I commented that if any of them wanted to contact me we could work something out. One individual did, and I helped her get started.

The man that was my first lead principal in this building had now moved downtown to the personnel position. I went to him for intervention to save me from this potential disaster. I trusted this guy to point me in the right direction. I asked him can he do anything for me. He was in charge of moving the chess pieces across the district, and knew who was going to retire and what was coming up. He suggested I fill out a voluntary transfer and specify the building in which they were going to start an alternative program the following school year. It would be for a male principal that I had respect for, and a female principal who previously had always been good to me. I will show you when this assignment ends how even people who smile in your face, can still be a backstabber. Isn't that an O'Jays song? He also advised that I approach this male principal in advance to make sure he would be okay with my transfer to his building, which I immediately did. I also found out it was going to be a co-teaching position with another male teacher. All in all, it sounded like my best choice. I filed the paper and the transfer went thru for the upcoming school year. An entirely new chapter of my career was about to take shape with some of the biggest challenges I had faced. Before that discussion, one more shocker from the principal from toga land:

An Administrator with no People Skills

At this point, one of the original three people who were there upon my arrival several years ago was coming up on retirement. He was a good guy that everyone liked. To say he could pass for Rodney Dangerfield's' brother was no exaggeration. We had gotten to know each other, and he just took care of people in general. On the very last day of his career on the clock, when students had already been let out for summer, and it was just administrators, the incredible happened.

Power had gone out in his neighborhood the previous night, and as a result he woke slightly late. He called and said he was on the way. Upon arrival, he explained to toga lady what had happened. She looked him dead in the eye, didn't flinch, and said, "You know how I feel about being late; you will have to take a ¼ sick day." This kind man who had worked in education 30 plus years was being told this on his LAST DAY. Thank God, he had the temerity to let her have it verbally. She huffed and puffed, and walked away. Readers, again, be aware of these administrators in big school systems. Often, they are incompetent, know less than you, and will do everything they can to manipulate your life. Don't let it happen! Appreciate the good ones.

Heartfelt Feelings of Frustration

It was about this time out of sheer frustration, I wrote the following piece as a means of therapy for myself. I never did anything with it. Now, in hindsight, I see that this perhaps was a precursor to what was going to happen to me in the next few years. Read and see if you agree:

I am an educator. At one time, that meant something. Unfortunately, it holds little of the value it once held.

As I approach the "middle years" of life, I, like many others, take a look at my career and evaluate its current state. I have been a teacher in an urban setting for my entire career, which in itself tends to put a few more "miles" on you than the average suburban setting. During this time, I have gone from your typical idealistic youngster to a grizzled vet who has seen and heard more than your everyday teacher will encounter in a lifetime. Pin a rose on me? Hardly, I am an urban educator, that's what I do.

I have watched countless children who come from backgrounds and experiences that no child deserves walk through the doors of my classroom. They find structure, routines, enthusiasm for learning, and most importantly compassion and warmth. Many respond favorably. This doesn't always show itself in black and white test scores, but in other subtle ways; a smile, where before was a scowl. I realize I impact children's lives.

Parental involvement continues to be a coveted entity. Often, we are reduced to a social service, where we are to meet more of these kids needs in a few hours a day then some parents manages to provide the remainder of the time.

Administrators continue to be a mystery. What happens to people, many of whom have spent minimal years of actual classroom time teaching, who suddenly become experts at what I do thru nothing more than the wonders of a master's degree? Worst yet are those administrators who during their tenure as teachers were average at best, now through the mystery of promotion find themselves qualified experts to refine those of us who have worked so very hard for so many years. Many of them mean well, but are caught up in the political cesspool that education has become, trapped between their superiors who demand more from those "incompetent teachers", and we who are actually in touch with kids, working with them on a day to day basis, year after year. Why is it that those who have very little contact with kids are the highly paid experts? What do I know, I'm just an educator.

Further, complicate all of this by the political arena which recently enacted the NCLB program which has virtually muddied the water for all urban educators who will forever be compared to test results from districts who have none of the hardships within that our children face daily in their lives, some generation after generation. As a direct result of this legislation, leaders within urban districts are forced to create new activities and responsibilities for already overworked teachers to employ, in order to justify to the state that we are doing all we can to correct these deficiencies.

Political correctness doesn't allow for the situation to be identified accurately. As long as the environment that our students come from remains the same, nothing will change. Poverty, ignorance, unhealthy environments, drugs and alcohol, low educational expectations, all have a direct and primary effect on the test scores our students produce. Does this mean educators give up? Not hardly. What it should mean is that those of us who have the experience of working in this environment directly with kids be allowed to make decisions we know benefit these kids and their education, regardless the outcome of one specific test. The life lessons along with all of the academic instruction that we accomplish is nothing short of miraculous, but yet it is overshadowed by the silly notion that one test reflects what we are accomplishing on a daily basis. But what do I know? I am just an educator.

Next, we are looking at a program that will require teachers to cover all subject matter, become expert at knowing the standards based education objectives for all of those areas, affecting state mandated minimum minutes of instruction due to the emphasis on reading and language, not to mention the scheduling nightmare involved, and be self-contained. This flies in the face of a middle school environment, and is nothing short of tunnel vision. Why? Yet again, those in power are able to make unilateral decisions regardless of the opinion of those who know; the educators. Along with this nightmare, we are now reminded that discipline expectations must be adjusted to reduce our suspension rates? In a population of 1000, if 20 or 25 are out at once, 975-980 are doing just fine. But that's not enough? Why? Those in power, removed from the daily struggle of working with difficult kids, lose focus and become delusional in what they consider fair expectations.

As a result, we are facing a crisis of huge proportion. Many veteran highly qualified staff are faced with looking elsewhere. Some would say good riddance. Others, who know better, realize that this results in a huge loss for our students. Meanwhile the question remains, why would a district sit back and allow this to happen? It could be that the most valuable resource within this system hasn't been included or consulted….. Educators.

The new school year would find me in another new building on the other side of town. The following segment will deal with the alternative assignment, the second year teaching 6th gr. Science, a new principal arrives, betrayal by a so-called friend, and the third year assignment when all hell breaks loose. But first – a pause for a chapter of bright happiness to illuminate some of this kick me sign circus.

CHAPTER 19

THE KICK ME SIGN FALLS OFF – FOR A MOMENT – I FIND LOVE

I would be remiss if I didn't take some time to share with you a moment where the kick me sign didn't win. My two kids born are the pride of my soul, and as long as I am alive, I will do anything for either of them. You remember I had endured a miserable divorce when they were 10 and 6. This was one of the most challenging moments of my life to get thru. I am grateful to God for his grace in enabling me to make it. I did some stupid stuff during that time, and he covered me. I had tried the dating scene, and it was awful. I had one brief time where I dated a gal and she helped me gain my self-esteem back. After that, I was convinced that I was going to grow old on my own.

Surprise! When I stopped looking, she found me. I went into the bank and the old cliché' of love at first sight is true. This sweet, beautiful lady with a bright smile and hearty laugh captured my heart. We had a great dating period in which we grew to love each other more and more. During my atrial fib attacks, she expected a call so she could join me at the hospital any time day or night. She was a loyal partner. We both had kids, her son was about my kids' age, and we knew a blended family would be a challenge. We didn't introduce our kids to each other until we were sure we wanted to make a go of it. In time, I asked her to marry me and she said yes. I had trust issues that she put at ease. Our saying to each other is inscribed on my ring, "together, forever, no matter what." Outside of a few bumps in the road the first year and a half of getting adjusted to this new life, it has been great. She brightens every day that she is in my life.

About a year and a half into our marriage, a real major scare invaded our new found happiness. My wife had found a lump in her breast. Upon further examination, she made an appointment. She is not one to go to doctors much, but this was different, it didn't feel right. Of course, even though it was in her body, my fears skyrocketed. This was the love of my life, my second chance at having peace and a partner for the second part of the ride of life, and now this monster had entered. She called me at work on her way home from the appointment in a state of shock. You have to know my wife, but she is a tough woman. For her to be in shock it buckled my knees and I listened. It turned out it was cancer and we were going to have to immediately go thru the process of being educated and deciding the best route for her.

I came home and found she stopped by her parents to let them know, and was waiting for me. I scooped her up and didn't want to let go. We sat and talked, cried, and I listened to her intently. All I could tell her was I am here for her every step of the way, and that God knows who she is, and we will have to trust in him. She had all the tests done, saw multiple doctors, went to different hospitals for second opinions, and consulted with her personal doctor for his advice. Everywhere we went, I gave everybody the third degree. I asked questions and got answers. I wanted an education, and I wanted the best for my wife. She had the biopsy. She then had a lumpectomy, along with lymph nodes removal. I lay awake at night listening to her breathing, just watching her. I begged God to spare her, that I could not take losing her. It was a frightening time. She decided upon radiation treatments and tamoxifen medicine for her after care treatments.

I want to say how proud I was and am of her. Not once did she complain, did she whine and say why me? She took on each step with bravery and kept on fighting. I am thankful for God's grace that he did spare her and it's been approximately nine years as of this writing with no reoccurrence of cancer. The kick me sign lost this battle!

Chapter 20

Move to a New Elementary Building and the Alternative World

This new program was designed to bring the worst behavior students who were on their last chance before expulsion to try and keep them in school. My partner and I were given free reign to do what we needed to make it work.

We had a 7th and 8th grade blended group that between the two of us we covered all the subject areas. A big part of the day was spent in keeping order and structure, establishing expectations and acceptable behaviors. It was almost impossible at times. These kids thought they were able to do whatever, whenever. We were the first two to stand united, with principal support, and tell them those days were over. We met with them and the parents in summer before school began to outline what was ahead. This was a big support for us because it eliminated a lot of misunderstandings when we would have to contact them for support. Although there were plenty of days where the stress and tension were brutal, I can look back at this time with a certain sense of pride.

My partner and I were recognized in the district as the force that caused this program to be successful. Our principal was proud of our efforts and said so. In addition, it was another time where I was free to be creative and actually draw on skills to build these kids up as well as teach them, without unfair administrative pressure coming down on the kick me sign. I firmly believe that I was able to plant some good seeds in these kids that others will be able to water and help grow later in their lives. Years later, I read in the paper where one of our students had been running the streets late one night and unfortunately had been shot. Thankfully, he recovered. I hope all others are well today.

Well, you would think given the accolades that were earned, we would remain in this program for a while. Oh no! The district in its wonderful wisdom decided to move the program to another building and start all over. Go figure. Neither my partner nor I had any interest in the new building so we gave it up.

The next year I was assigned to work as a 6th grade science teacher. This was fine with me. It was a subject I was comfortable with teaching. Earlier, I mentioned that large urban districts, who are always desperately trying to raise test scores against all odds, often bring in the newest programs supposedly designed to raise those scores. One of them was in the beginning stages in science district wide. I walked in completely unprepared or briefed on the material or what was expected. Surprised?

Let me say, I am old school in that reading, comprehension, drill and practice, memorization, are all skills needed to exist in the world. Unfortunately, this is what will get you looked at as a dinosaur that needs to be put out to pasture. This new plan completely centered on experiments. Can you believe it? This is fine, if the other parts are in place, and you are in a district where discipline is not an issue. Otherwise, imagine the fun you have when you are trying to plan, prepare, and implement lessons that center on experiments by kids who have very little self-control and no fear of consequences by the school for their discipline issues. Needless to say, difficult is an understatement. As the year continued, I adapted and progress began. I had not one negative word towards me by any administrator, so I felt all was well. I forgot the KICK ME sign!

As the year drew to a close, the male administrator announced he was retiring. He was and is a good man. Nobody wanted him to leave. Often, change brings about some good, but other times, change brings problems. This was one of those times. I will give you the ugly details in the next chapter, my third year in this building. I was approached and told that I was being moved from my position. Sound familiar? There was no reason given other than there was an opening that my certification could fill – 5th grade. Also, a teacher who was going to be laid off had certification that he could use in my science position. On first read, you might say that makes sense. Until you find out that this guy had one year seniority against my thirteen in the district, and that his license could have filled the same 5th grade spot I was being moved to. Not so good now huh.

I began my immediate investigation as the year concluded, and prepared to do what I could to not go to the fifth grade. See, I was thinking ahead, and realized that since our school expected elementary classes to be self-contained, this was going to be a huge problem. Two more of those big savior programs that were flops had been instituted in the district, one was America's Choice in Math, and one was the literacy collaborative. I had ZERO training in either area, and ZERO experience teaching either area. One would think the best interest of kids would be to not put a teacher in that position which inevitably sets the teacher up for failure, and indirectly the kids as well. That is, unless of course, there is a hidden agenda behind the move. Guess what? The kick me sign with a bulls eye was glowing neon on my back and I didn't know it. What was ahead was far worse than I could have imagined.

CHAPTER 21

NEW ASSIGNMENT, NEW PRINCIPAL, FINAL STRAW

A TRAGIC LOSS

efore I go any further, I want to stop and remember a student I had in sixth grade. This girl was fun. Big smile, tons of energy and always checking me with questions that made me think. We established a relationship that was solid. She lived with mom, step-dad, and siblings nearby. One night, a fire broke out and mom and siblings were lost, along with this bright young girl. When we were notified, it knocked the wind out of me. Not another student lost! Some teachers go thru a whole career and never endure any losses like this. I had a few now, and it wasn't getting any easier. I attended her funeral, along with the majority of the city. The images and the heartbreak remain today. Such a horrible tragedy leaves a mark.

Two years earlier, right before I came to this school, another student had been killed in a random drive by shooting when he was in his home. He was 11 years old. It seems like this school had a dark cloud above it.

Over the summer, I continued to email my immediate supervisor the previous year to see if she had asked for this change. She constantly said no. When the new principal came on board, I began to contact her. My angel principal in the meantime had left her previous beautiful suburban spot and returned to the high school in town, because she "just has a thing for these kids". I asked her if she lost her mind, that's how good the suburban school was that she moved to. Anyway, this new principal at my building was a former assistant of hers at the high school.

Because of my concerns, I felt free to email her and introduce myself, along with explaining my problem with the new assignment and my reasoning. Along with this, I mentioned how my previous supervisor insisted that she had not requested this change for me, so of course I was wondering where this was coming from. Our emails were totally professional, but in the end, the new assignment was going to happen. What I didn't know, was this lady was the type that didn't like to be questioned. She had been taking these emails the wrong way, as if I was challenging her authority, which was completely not true. Apparently, my previous supervisor was not completely forthcoming with me. The recommendation for me to take that spot did not come from the new principal. Summer was over, and the third year in this building was about to begin, and it would prove to be one that almost brought me to the end of the career prematurely. The experiences of the 5th grade follow.

Chapter 22

5th Grade Again – A Different World

What a difference a different building and administrator can make with any specific grade level. I had to start the year with the knowledge that the circumstances with my assignment that involved my former supervisor was suspect. When you have known someone for a lot of years, trusted them, and then this happens, it is hard to swallow. The year was spent at a distance, and she knew that I knew. Our professional friendship was never the same.

The new boss had taken the emails as a sign of arrogance on my part, and was not happy. The kick me sign had doubled in size. As always, my colleagues in the hall quickly saw me as a trusted veteran. My classroom as always was in control and on task. See, when an administrator has decided you have crossed some imaginary line, nothing you do will change that. You might as well put your guard up, and do what you can to protect yourself.

Rather than bore you with all the minor details, the area she focused on was the two areas I had no training or experience in. Surprised? So was I. This was an evaluation year. The one area she "attempted" to help was by assigning the "math coach" to "help". Now there is a gig if you can get it. The help was once a week coming in and teaching a lesson. The rest of the program was on me to absorb all the while teaching and trying to survive. The other area she decided to "postpone" my teaching it for me to prepare for next year. How? I have no idea. But somehow, she used the fact that she felt I wasn't prepared to teach it next year that at the year-end evaluation she wrote me up. Mind you, in my career, NEVER, had any principal given a negative evaluation. The basis was in the one area I hadn't shown enough growth, NONSENSE, and in the other area I was being stubborn and not willing to prepare.

The truth is she offered no assistance in that area. I had told her that this year was as difficult as I knew it would be and had prepared her for. She maintained she can assign positions as she saw fit. The new boss used the emails from summer to indicate in my evaluation my stubborn attitude. She appeared to be holding a grudge, which my union rep even pointed out. I did everything to make this go away folks. I almost humiliated myself by begging for her forgiveness. All to no avail. She was focused, and I knew if I didn't do something, the following year I was going to be looking for a job courtesy of this angry lady. My stress level was at an all-time high. My physical issues were getting worse. This principal was relentless. She had taken a veteran with all tremendous evaluations and reduced him to nothing. This is the dark side of our business. The only thing I knew to do was reach out to my union. The following gives you some insight to that issue:

Union Disappointment

I had always been raised a union guy. In the steel factory, you had strength in your union. Administration would never dare to pull this kind of nonsense on employees. I will tell you now, put very little faith in your union. On this matter, they did enough to keep her at arm's length. But ultimately, we ended up in HR with a lady who openly commented that teachers are lazy and resistant to change. My three year stretch in this building had come to an end. This boss had shown her cards in what was in store for me next year. All I could do was put in for a voluntary transfer.

Guess what? Over the summer, the transfer was rejected by the superintendent. He soon resigned under a storm of controversy after being there one year. As summer progressed, and the new superintendent took over, my union actually came through on this occasion. They showed him the history of what had occurred and the fact that I was entitled to that transfer. Thank God again, this guy saw the facts and allowed me to transfer. The principal ended up back at the high school where the district felt she was a better fit. The following year the district eliminated her husband's created position in the district so she resigned and went back to her hometown area. All I can say is bye- bye.

Petty and Vindictive

Just to show you how she was, she would see me at school functions and walk right by me, look me in the eye, and never say a word. You would think I had committed some grave personal offense to her. I personally believe she was angry that her intentions to nail me failed and that I survived.

I would be remiss if I failed to mention a couple incidents with other staff that supports my premise this building was an unhealthy atmosphere run by this woman. A lady, who was talented and taught a third grade class, had come down to her last year till retirement. She was more than ready to go. As Christmas break approached, she mentioned how awful this year had been. With the new leadership, the lack of discipline, and the directives from higher administration it was all getting to be too much. On the last day before break she said good bye it's been good working with you. I was stunned. I said well you will be back to finish the year right? She responded she just couldn't take it anymore, she was done. I reminded her of all the sick time she had accumulated that she would lose if she quit prematurely as well as a very large severance check. Again, her response was it isn't worth it, I am done. She never came back. How sad a veteran's career comes down to complete exhaustion, and frustration. Without any recognition for a job well done, they just disappear.

I didn't realize how relevant that was to me and how I would deal with a similar problem in the near future. My teaching partner here was a sweet lady with many years of experience. She was a great teacher and friend. One day she broke down in tears in front of the kids, they had driven her to that point. Another lady down the hall, had a full out blowout with the principal. It was just a toxic environment that was claiming its victims. This was also the place that I was reminded of all the dirty laundry that happens behind the scenes that rarely is exposed. It was quickly losing focus, and people were dropping left and right. A lady across the hall, outstanding teacher, and one around the corner, also felt the wrath of this principal. Again, amazing how some people with no people skills become administrators.

Chapter 23

Kick Me Sign Tries Again – A Big Scare for Me

It was about this time that I had been noticing an increase in discomfort in my abdomen area that sometimes would give me pain in the chest as well. I had been through so much already I didn't want to even give it a thought that something could be wrong. It just wouldn't let up over quite a period of time. Finally, I went to the doctor and he ordered some tests.

He found that my gallbladder didn't look right. There was stuff in it and stones that shouldn't be there. The bad part was if any of the stones were to dislodge and enter the duct, there would be pain off the charts and emergency surgery that would be needed. He sent me to a specialist. This guy did some further examination and tests. He concluded that he saw bumps in the gallbladder that usually indicate cancer. He was pretty cold about it, but needless to say it knocked me for a loop. I read up and found that gallbladder cancer was pretty serious, and not an easy one to survive. After everything that had happened already, now this?

My faith was certainly being tested. I had to stay focused and trust that God had this in control. The surgery was scheduled. I asked how I will know if you found cancer. He told me I would wake up with a tube down my nose and a urine catheter still in place with a major incision running down the middle of my abdomen. He would have to determine while in surgery if anything had went to the liver or pancreas and do some removing of parts of those organs

"

if it had. If I didn't have cancer, it was a laparoscopic procedure, relatively easy to recover from. A very uncomfortable way to go to sleep before surgery. I looked at him moments before and said "take care of me" as I grabbed his hand. Instantly, it went dark. As I woke up in recovery, the first thing I did was grab for my nose to see if there was a tube. NO TUBE! Thank God again for his grace and mercy to spare me from any cancer. The kick me sign lost again!

Three Years of Grace

It was around this time that I found myself returning to church. Many years earlier in my life, I was part of a church that ended up being one that was out of control. The problem quite simply was the pastor had built this "empire" where he was the final authority and nobody told him no. What had started out as a great Christian church deteriorated to this ugly reality. I left this under great duress, and vowed I would never have anything to do with church again. I never turned my back on God; however, I did no longer have use for the structure of church, and the hypocritical nature of people. Through all of the events you have read so far, I leaned heavily on my faith to sustain me.

I had my kids going to a local church for kids' activities. I felt I owed that church to at least attend a service or two. During that time, I found myself attracted to the style of message being delivered by the pastor. I remained skeptical, but open to listen. In time, I realized he was a solid person who could be trusted. His compassion for people was the convincing element. Soon, he picked up and moved. I was frustrated. Never again I said. I learned quickly "never say never."

Several years later, he returned to the area upon invitation of others who were drawn to his ministry and were hoping he could come and start up a church of his own. He began meeting in a local school building and within weeks the numbers of attendance were huge. I heard he was back, and the second week of his return, I attended. I could not deny that this was something I wanted to be part of.

Over the next three years, we grew in size and moved to our new location, which was a huge empty building in a local strip mall. I became part of the sound ministry and drama performances. I grew very close to this pastor, and we became friends. Then, just as suddenly it had started, it came to an end. It turns out this time the people who were the "leaders" of the church started to nitpick him on everything. He finally had enough, and retired. I was crushed and angry. Knowing what they had done to this guy, I wanted nothing to do with the new set up and I immediately stopped attending.

Faith is central to my existence. I do not however know if I will be a part of another church again. This is for God to decide. Fortunately, I have kept in touch with this pastor and he remains my friend and counselor. So, in the end, all was not lost.

THE JOURNEY IS ALMOST OVER

The school year ended and my transfer had placed me in what was perceived to be the best K-8 building in town. It used to be before the district allowed open enrollment within town so that kids from all over town could go there. At that point, it went downhill. Unfortunately, nobody had told me that. I was given a choice of 8th gr. Science and the lead principal, who I had worked with at the original middle school building, described what the job would entail. It sounded very good. Guess what? It turned out not to be that way, and when I mentioned that to the new boss that was my new supervisor, he said we were going to do things the way he saw fit.

The new boss by the way was an older male, and a big guy. You will hear more about him later. The other principal was a lady who had been my former teaching partner who I went to lunch with every day, shared stories with her, and attended her wedding. Unfortunately, she never used any pull she had to help me at this building. The previous bad evaluation was trying to follow me thru this man's ignorance of our contract. After his insistence, the union again intervened and had the superintendent verify that the old evaluation was now moot.

Thankfully, this year was a non-evaluation year, so I was able to try and focus on learning the new grade level and subject area once again without fears of administrative bias and evaluations. The new year was set to begin. This would be my 28th year in education. This would also be the year that my very existence would be challenged. This would be the year I stared enormous adversity in the face and wondered if I would survive. Please, read on to see this destructive year that I was about to begin:

Chapter 24

My Last Building Assignment – Impending Doom

As always, I went into the building early to prepare and get acquainted with materials. The science curriculum was the same bad program I had in the sixth grade class, just now the eighth grade version. The hands on stuff you can imagine now with older kids was even a bigger issue. Factor in the lack of support over discipline issues, and you realize quickly it was a bad idea. I checked with the guy who taught the previous year and he told me he rarely ever did experiments because it turned into a big out of control mess. I was not surprised to hear that. I shared with him what I had in mind and he said that it sounded good to him. The year begins.

There aren't enough textbooks for all the students I had so we worked without them, which is no easy task. I started building rapport, and structure in the classroom with the kids, for the most part fairly well. The shocker was the discipline was far worse than the previous building and the support even less. Quickly found that the previous year or two, it had disintegrated. It was a shame folks, this was a new building, full of up to date technology with beautiful classrooms. If somebody had the nerve to build a plan to show the kids who was in charge, the accomplishments would have been great. The truth is the district had begun to adopt an attitude of "understanding" our kids and simply not "punishing" them. The truth is one of the only points we could count on in the state report card was attendance. If kids were out of school suspended, the attendance went down and we risked losing that one point we were able to get. They just wouldn't have it that we could come up with 0 points.

My unit principal was quite a character. I want to say up front upon meeting him he would impress you as a nice guy. As you began to get to know him, he was a little complex. This district is notorious for putting people into administrative positions that go along with any district directive without question. He fit that bill. Somehow, he was known in the district I believe for working there years ago. He had gone on to business I believe, had worked in another district, and may have retired to be rehired here in this district. He was your classic fence rider. He could sit with you and chat like an old buddy, all the while knowing his game plan. Downtown dictates everything, he would smile to your face in potential agreement on something, only to turn around and do what downtown said no matter what. One day I noticed the superintendent coming out of his office. This was quite unusual. So I jokingly said to him, "Are you in trouble?" He smiled and told me not at all, in fact, he had gone to school with the superintendent and they were friends. Isn't that nice? It turns out his wife worked in the building as a secretary. She had a commanding personality and you were better off to not make her irritated. Interesting that the district frowns on married folk working in the same building but had made exception for them.

In any event, the year started. I could see early that the good reputation of this building was inaccurate; the kids were out of control. In the back of my mind, I thought that it was good we have an African American male administrator that they will respect. That too was inaccurate. One has to be firm and back up your words with kids. He was another one who believed in lots of warnings and giving kids plenty of chances. Students used this to their advantage. Some, to the point where they openly mocked him and got away with it. It was a shame. The staff begged him to do something about it. The old smiling conversation would occur and nothing changed except getting worse.

The negative evaluation from last year that the superintendent had bypassed with my new assignment caught his attention.

Normally, the evaluation would require multiple evaluations the next year. He expressed his intent to do that with me. Of course, that was unacceptable, and fortunately this was one rare occasion where the union stepped up and intervened. Fortunately, the superintendent agreed and negated the need for further evaluation. After all, the evaluation dealt with falsely perceived literacy and math instruction deficits. I was teaching SCIENCE. This illustrates big guy's focus on whatever policy says he will do regardless of the circumstances. Before I forget, here is a little story to share with you:

Unbelievable Nonsense

One day a friend and I were outside with bus duty at the end of the day on the primary side. Things were almost done, when a little 2ⁿᵈ grader started a ruckus. The teacher called for a principal. The lady who was my former teaching partner came out. We were there for support. It turns out the little guy had a gun in his book bag. The principal began to plead and baby this little one to give her the gun. He refused. I was thinking I would simply bend down and take the book bag. She continued and finally the little guy conceded. I asked my friend if it would be swept under the rug. He said if the gun had come out and we both were shot in the forehead with blood gurgling, the district would inquire what we did wrong and let the incident go! Of course, he was being silly, but you get the drift. By the way, I heard and saw nothing of the incident again aside from a meeting held with the parents in the school. Hard to imagine?

My physical and mental state had begun early to deteriorate from all the incredible strain this environment produced on teachers. I had to take sick time frequently, and when that happens you realize how bad it hurts you. In these big urban districts, you rarely get subs that follow your plan, and in fact leave you worse than what you left them. It's hard to blame them. They are underpaid and they are easy targets for out of control kids. They get little support from principals, and basically are on their own to survive the day. That said, there are certain things that are unacceptable. One is for the sub to undermine the teacher in any way shape or form.

When I came back from one of these days off, the one class that was half way decent was out of control. This is very unusual. I investigated with those I could rely on and they responded the teacher said we shouldn't do the stuff I had left for them, it was a waste! I was enraged. I went immediately to the principal who basically back-pedaled and tried to make excuses for her. I told him it was unacceptable and didn't want her back in my room. He then said it was his decision to make and he thought she was fairly good in the class. As the year continued, this same sub caused problems in most every room she covered. Many teachers complained and FINALLY he could see it wasn't working. One day he actually verbally put her in her place. After that, she went on to sub at the high school. Imagine, the old veteran teacher was right.

This environment was so toxic to teachers it was causing breakdowns left and right. When I arrived, there was an opening that still hadn't been filled. Apparently, the teacher from last year who was a young teacher had gotten to the point with his 7th grade students that he just couldn't deal with it anymore. Before the year was out, he called it quits. He went to his part time job and said he'd rather just get by than have to deal with the disrespect, violence, and no support from administration.

They hired a lady with experience of a few years a couple months into the school year. She was mild mannered and made the mistake that many make by trying to win students over by being their buddy. Her classroom control evaporated. You could see the panic and stress on her face every day. The kids ruled her room. It was inevitable that her and the principal would eventually bump heads. At first, she had a way of just looking like she was glazed over and the noise from her room was terrible. They would disrespect her in the hallways as well. The teacher did the thing that you learn not to do in this environment and that was to reach out to the principal with any frequency. He was the type that would walk thru and offer lip service in terms of trying to help gain control of the class, but then leave you to yourself. The kids ignored what he said, and continued to devour the lady. Finally, the confrontation occurred when some kids complained to the principal about her. She was called in and he verbally knocked her down, leaving her with the feeling that the problem was her and not the kids. It was the final straw. As I recall, this occurred early in the week, and she resigned effective the first Friday after the discussion, even with no new job to go to.

So now the kids who were out of control, got a teacher and drove her out, were back to no regular teacher again. They filled the room by asking special education people to cover along with subs on a regular basis, no further hires came along. Obviously, the student learning for that group was seriously impacted.

Substitute Abuse

One day I was walking to the door to go home. A male sub, who was one of the best we had, came around the corner with a dazed, confused look on his face. I inquired if he was okay. He said he was just punched in the gut by a fourth grader while he was helping on dismissal. I asked what the teachers did to help. He said their response was "that's the way he is." Sadly, the real truth is the kid had been in so much trouble with no consequences, they knew it was meaningless to try and get something done. The sub was out of luck.

Daily Chaos takes its Toll

A couple more incidents to share to illustrate this horrible environment. One day, a lady across the hall who was one of the better teachers, came out of her room crying as kids came in for the day. She walked across to an empty room. I went to check on her. She simply had a brief breakdown that day due to the normal stress that she was going to have to face again. I comforted her and wondered how this was ever going to get better. My conditions were getting worse, and the anxiety started to grow with the partner of depression, who I had yet to realize its huge existence.

A male teacher across the hall was also very good. He had similar years of experience, and we became friends. He was a very relaxed guy, much like me. He too, was blown away by how bad things had gotten. He would repeatedly ask in meetings what we are doing to resolve these problems. He would continually get shot down by the principal and his double speak. You could see the irritation begin to grow. One day, while in my room during class change, I heard this horrible bellowing in the hall. Here the man came with a student who he had tried to settle down who responded with an F U. This was the final straw. Red-faced, he was bellowing and bringing the kid down the hall to be seen by the principal. Of course, long story short, next to nothing happened. The pressure cooker continued.

A female teacher who was slightly older taught a few doors down. Stories kept coming back how badly things had gotten in her room. She was old school, as I, and expected respect to be shown. It never was. Her teaching became a sad thing to see. She would stand and try to do her lesson, while nobody was listening. She assigned something and she would get flak about why do we need to do this from the kids. I could see it taking a toll on her, and she too inquired what are we going to do? It seemed she was considered a complainer and basically ignored.

A veteran female teacher who had physical disabilities was also starting to crumble. The administration had little mercy. She was being negatively evaluated as I was before, except in her case, it was continuing. Can you imagine having the gall to see a person who is physically debilitated trying to do her best and still make her life further miserable by this degrading negative evaluation pressure? It was a shame. Her class was on task, and normally quiet. That alone should have earned her some consideration. It began to destroy her as well. She filed for disability retirement for her physical major problems as well as depression. Thankfully, finally, it was granted, and she escaped with her dignity. God bless her, I hope she is well.

Finally, one day a sweet lady who had become my friend by

being a special education teacher who worked with me for a couple of inclusion classes reached her breaking point. She came in my room frantic and crying. No kids were present so I had her sit and relax. She shared with me that she once again had been asked to fill in for the older lady a few doors down who had taken sick time. This meant she would have to teach the whole day subject matter she obviously had not prepared, and do so alone without help. First of all, it is not their job to do that. I should never be asked to fill in for a special education teacher when I am not qualified to do so. The same was with her situation. She was crying and saying she just couldn't take it anymore, she can't do it. The pressure cooker was now starting to boil over. I suggested she tell the principal either someone else does it, or she felt sick and needed to go home. Thankfully, another person was chosen to do the fill in for the day. My friend was relieved but embarrassed that she had broken down. I told her she isn't the first and I am sure won't be the last.

A male who had been teaching for some time and was well respected in the system had repeatedly tried in staff meetings to get change in place. He was constantly rebuffed. One night, he reached his breaking point. During parent teacher conferences, when the room was empty, he and the principal crossed paths. It became verbally heated and loud. I walked over and closed the door so attention wouldn't be drawn. After some time the administrator came out and walked away. I checked on the teacher who said he finally had enough and they had it out. For the moment, it seemed to help the teacher. In the long run, nothing changed. The teacher's frustrations remained. Thankfully, at the end of this school year we were in, he got a job in a wonderful suburban district where he is happy, and appreciated.

I would hope by now it is clear to see the toxic environment I have referred to frequently. It was not just me, or my ill – perceived lack of ability. It affected all of us. Some were able to sustain the best they could. Others, reached a breaking point and weren't able to stay. Little did I know that my existence and future was about to change dramatically. The kick me sign was about to deliver the biggest boot yet.

Chapter 25

Tragedy Strikes Again

Before I continue to share about my personal issues that were soon to come, I need to pause and share with you one of the worst things I ever saw in my career. Word spread quickly one evening that a great tragedy had occurred with some of our student population in the district. The news quickly covered the story. Apparently, several students who had been out late at night were driving along a relatively quiet side road early the next morning. The driver lost control, went off the road, flipped upside down, and landed in a pond. Sadly, all but two were killed. When I tell you that this dark cloud consumed everyone in our district, I exaggerate not. This was brutal. It turns out; one of the kids was a student I had earlier in the year. He was one of those who would get into trouble frequently, but had established a good relationship with me. He was a likeable kid, who enjoyed sports as I do, and had this big infectious smile. He had left our building to go to a different one due to all the trouble he had been in our location. This was a brutal loss for me to get around. I really was devastated. Funerals were being held around town by the various families. I attended this young guy's service. I looked at him in the casket and was blown away by the fact that just recently he and I were laughing and telling a story. Now, his life snuffed out way too early, and he was gone. You just don't get over some things. This was one of them.

CHAPTER 26

MY FINAL STRAW — THE BREAKING POINT IS HERE

The first year in this building was now a few months till the end. It was by far the most difficult year I had experienced. In hindsight, I now see it was an accumulative effect that was now swallowing me up. The stress was starting to take its toll. The pressure and tension of the stress was starting to exacerbate physical conditions I have to the point of great concern.

Throughout my career, one of the things I was most proud of was my ability to maintain an organized, on task, civil classroom with the majority of students respecting me as a man and as their teacher. This has to exist in order for learning to occur. You have seen you basically have yourself to depend on to get the job done, since the majority of administrators are so busy covering their own backsides for downtown that they throw the teachers, young and old, into the fire and feel let them figure it out.

It was about this time, I could feel the control and the respect factor starting to lesson for the first time. I had been tested by the toughest in the other district, but now these kids were approaching a new level. It was about this time when a female student crossed the line. She made a big circus in the classroom and challenged my authority, demanding why I was having them work a particular assignment, claiming she wasn't learning anything, and stomping out of the room. I attempted to pursue her to calm her down since I had my special education teacher in the room. She was determined this was going to be her stand. I told her "for not learning anything" she was doing pretty well, getting a good grade in my class. We returned and she continued to try and get the class fired up with her in a basic move to overthrow the control of the class for them to take over. I know it sounds crazy, but that was exactly what happened. I had never felt so disgusted about my job.

I tried to get to see the principal over the next day or two, but he always postponed. Finally, he said to stop by. Upon presenting my detailed recount of the blowup, he very calmly said "How did that make you feel?!" Can you imagine? I was enraged, and completely devastated. At this point in my life and career, a teenager had gotten over on me and a principal seemed to be supporting it, redirecting the attention back to me rather than what he would do with the student.

Something inside me snapped. I was in a perilous state at that moment, and I was scared. I went to the hallway, and was staring out the window, when that male I told you before who ended up in a better system, came walking by. He asked if I was okay. I said "no actually I am not." He said, "I could tell, I've been there myself." He asked if I would like a recommendation of somebody I could talk to. He explained that when he reached that point before, he went to this doctor and he was a tremendous help. I said sure. He gave me his card. I called and made an appointment.

The next day I took a sick day and over the weekend, I received an email from the principal who came into work on a Saturday to send it to me. He wanted me to stop by Monday morning, he wanted to talk. It turns out his plan was to assign two people to come to my room and work with me on managing my classroom time so that I could be teaching what the district was expecting and how to block out the time. This essentially supported the student's disrespectful allegations of my not teaching relevant material.

Can you imagine how insulted I was? In addition, he had managed to maneuver a way to get into my class for evaluative purposes, since he was going to join them. The whole hallway was going crazy, but yet he chose to make an example out of one of the most well managed rooms in the building. I taught EVERYTHING

I was supposed to be teaching every day! He wasn't even that familiar with the curriculum yet. As I read this email, I bottomed out. I started feeling the walls closing in, and I had to do something. My union was no help at all. Their excuse was he could do what he was doing, no matter that he was being arbitrary and singling out somebody for harassment. These two people were those who would do exactly what they had been told to do with me. I had taught longer than either of them, and neither had any experience with older kids. Their "help" would be to crash course me in things I already knew and disappear. Then, the door would be open for the principal to start slowly going thru the process of monitoring me to see if I was installing the new game plan to the tee or I believe my time would be short. Something was not right, and I was scared. I needed help. I had bottomed out, the last straw, and didn't know what to do. I did know, I couldn't do this anymore.

Chapter 27

My First Trip to a Psychiatrist

I went to the appointment. I had not been back to school since the call off. It had been a few days. I was really having a bad go of it. My brains seemed scrambled, my nerves were shot. I couldn't sleep, couldn't keep a focused thought. I called out to God for help numerous times, and knew he was there, but the cloud of darkness was surrounding over this brewing storm. After a psychological work-up, he determined that I needed to get away from my job right away. He said "you are the sickest patient I have" and "I am concerned about your health." He also recommended I go on two anti-depressants right away as well as maintain an anti-anxiety medication. It is a little disconcerting to hear that from a psychiatrist, but of course I was in a very fragile state and followed his directions. Also, it makes you wonder if a pending disaster was coming or was it averted. During that consultation, I told him how strange this whole feeling is and he said something that helped me settle. He said, "Most people when they reach their breaking point, ignore it, and go on until it's too late. You at least realized you were at the end of your breaking point, and you came for some help. We will work to get you better." Thank God, once again my prayers were answered by this genuine doctor. Now, I needed to go thru the political red tape minefield of following procedures to take care of myself. The next section breaks down the basics of what needed to happen, and then finishes with the final kick in the butt of what the union did in the end.

Chapter 28

Following the Yellow Brick Road

It was mid-March, and I submitted paperwork to begin FMLA immediately per doctor's recommendation. I didn't return to school through the end of the school year. I had to use remaining sick time during this leave if I expected to get paid. For this reason, we had a sick bank that people contribute days to in the event they have a major illness event during which they would use up all sick time which is what had happened with my situation. They are then supposed to apply to the bank committee requesting an amount of days that would serve as a bridge to get them thru the financial crisis.

I consulted with union reps and followed procedure. This process was initially denied. In case you didn't read it right, it was DENIED. My paperwork from the doctor said "This was a matter of life and death." These three teachers and one administrator of the committee in their unknown reasoning decided that's not good enough and denied what was rightfully mine. Keep in mind, sick time was gone now and for the month of April I had no income. The district takes what you have built up to pay you for the summer at regular rate and through a formula, deduct all days you had no pay, combine it with what you've already earned, and reduce it. This equated to me taking home less than 50% of what I normally made. This should not have been necessary. When questioned, they said this should be covered by disability as an excuse why they weren't granting what was rightfully mine. I was enraged. Who were they to dictate what I should do? How do they know I wasn't going to do that anyway, and what does that have to do with their responsibility to pay me what I have earned as a bridge till things are ironed out?

This did nothing but further worsens my state of mind and caused my physical issues to debilitate to a perilous state. At this point, I began the process of filing for disability. Keep in mind that nobody on the union committee had the integrity to show me in their guidelines that once an applicant for sick bank time has applied for disability the committee will grant the applicant sick bank days automatically as needed. This was due to my original premise that these sick days existed as a bridge till disability would start or else the person would have to do something else.

I filed again with the sick bank according to their new instructions. I followed it to a tee. They denied me again! I filed for an appeal. I had to sit with the union president, the committee chair, and the superintendent for the hearing. Now, doesn't that seem a bit odd to you? Don't you feel that my reps are actually being pitted against me and in conjunction with administration? I did too. First, I was asked to wait in the lobby for a few minutes while the three of them went into the room. They then invited me in. I presented to the superintendent and they said their piece. I left and waited for the outcome. Guess what? It was DENIED. It was approaching summer now, and by my psychiatrist's advice, I continued seeking disability retirement. I also requested the guidelines by which this committee operates. See, those are never provided unless you ask. Their meetings are always closed, and their discussion is never revealed. Their final ruling is very brief and hazy. Going into summer, my only hope was that the STRS would see fit to grant this disability retirement to save my life. The kick me sign weighed heavily on my back as summer began, I was financially in desperate means, and we started the process.

Chapter 29

Dealing with the STRS and Their Process

I continued seeing my psychiatrist and realized it was most necessary to continue doing that for help. One of the things I discovered early was that I accepted the condition of being wound up tight as a drum, insomnia, irritability, lack of energy, a variety of issues, etc. as just a normal way of life. In fact, it was far from normal. I realized it was a defense mechanism that had grown to help me survive these unbearable ordeals. Remember, there are many teachers who go to work every day with excitement and joy at what they do for a living. I no longer was one of those people, and vaguely remembered being one. We quickly determined that when FMLA had run out, there was no way I could return to work and hope to survive. Sadly, along with my physical ailments and mental state, the doctor diagnosed me with severe depression. This was devastating to me, since I was one of those folks who always prided himself on his intellect. I didn't realize that depression has nothing to do with intellect and in fact is a condition that is as devastating as any severe medical condition. Thankfully, this doctor was familiar with the STRS system. The system is the state teacher retirement system and all the governing factors that go with it under their control.

We were now entering August, and time was running out. Options were very limited as to what I could do. I had some FMLA days left that my doctor submitted a letter for me to start the new year on until they were exhausted, hoping by that point we had heard from STRS. I knew if we didn't, tough times were ahead. I would have to go on unpaid medical leave, try to find some way to survive financially, and make a decision of what to do with my life. I was 54, still a year away from retirement, and I knew nothing but teaching as a career. I had a brief stint as a business owner/manager, but those opportunities were gone. To say I was in a frantic state is a gross understatement. After another appointment with my psychiatrist, he sent a letter to the medical board asking for our case to receive a quicker look if possible due to my condition and his resolve that I could in no way return to work without seriously jeopardizing my health and possibly life.

Thank God, we received a response that indicated their agreement and an appointment to see their independent psychiatrist for corroboration. We were now just a few short weeks away from opening of the new school year. My appointment was set for a Monday morning about an hour north of my home. I drove there feeling an enormous weight of what this appointment meant to my life.

Chapter 30

The Moment of Truth – Meeting the STRS Doctor

There is a certain stigma our society puts on people who are seeking the help of a psychiatrist. I was guilty of that to a certain degree as well. I entered the appointment with a little embarrassment of being there. The doctor and staff were quite professional and made me comfortable. I then went into the room with the doctor and endured an examination interview of about an hour. Afterwards, I was put thru a series of computer psychiatric tests designed for quick feedback and diagnosis to use along with the doctor's exam, to determine my state of mind. This took about 2 ½ hours to complete. It was exhausting but necessary. Afterwards, I spoke with the doctor again. He knew time was critical so he instructed his secretary to fax the results the next day. I thanked them for the time and left, not knowing what was going to happen.

Later, I found out that the medical review board received the test results and the doctor's recommendation that corroborated my psychiatrist's recommendation for disability on Wednesday. They reviewed it and presented it to the decision committee on Thursday and it was approved. They sent out the paperwork on Friday notifying me and the district of their decision that I received on that Saturday. The new school year was due to start the very next week! I believe to this day God accelerated the process so I could be relieved of all the stress of not knowing what was going to happen to me.

Credit for a Job well Done

I do want to take a moment and give credit to the STRS and their people. They are one of the most efficient organizations I have ever dealt with thru this process. Their people are very helpful, bright, and informed of their business they take care of. I never felt disrespected, like I did with my own union "brothers" and they always answered all my questions thoroughly. This book has enough people in it that didn't do their jobs, or used their jobs for their own personal power trip. The STRS is not one of them. Kudos to the organization for a job well done. Thank you.

CHAPTER 31

THE CRAZY RIDE SLOWS DOWN AND COMES TO AN END

The long and sometimes crazy journey had come to an end. It certainly was a whirlwind. The career itself at times looked like it would never end. Then, before I knew it, my kids were grown and married, I had my master's degree in administration that I never was able to use, through a series of degrading, depleting incidents I had been pushed to the brink of a meltdown, knew I needed professional help, and sought it out. The result was the doctors and the state agreed that I had a lot of problems, with depression being the main catalyst to making everything else worse. I had walked thru the minefield of red tape and I was now classified on disability retirement.

In one of my favorite movies, "Mr. Holland's Opus," Richard Dreyfuss' character was given a hero's goodbye in the finale of the movie. I always had this notion that somebody would put together some wonderful goodbye party that I could always remember in my golden years. The time had come and I didn't even have anyone open the door for me. The previous year ended, the new year began, and I was just gone.

After working your entire adult life and becoming used to the routines that the work required of you on a daily basis, that was quite an adjustment. I still had this dogma of having depression hanging on me, so I really didn't want people to know my business. So basically, like an old cowboy, I just faded into the sunset. I found most people didn't know what had happened to me. Some found out that I was on disability retirement, but that was about it. Sad to say, very few people reached out to check on me. That is quite a wake- up call that humbles you, making you realize how many friends you actually have versus how many acquaintances. I now set my mind towards getting healthy again.

I needed to follow every direction of the doctor and abide by the STRS rules of disability retirement. The biggest challenge is the realization of how completely consumed I had become with depression and anxiety over the conditions that I had suffered through all these years. It was scary to know how close I had become to being in a very serious predicament, and I was grateful, promising God that I would use this time to get healthy again, grow older gracefully, be available to my family and find my smile again. For the first time in a very long time, the kick me sign didn't seem to weigh much anymore.

CHAPTER 32

THE KICK ME SIGN GETS ONE LAST BOOT - BY THE UNION

had always been the kind of person that when I perceive an injustice has occurred, it irritates me so bad that I do everything I can to make those involved own up to their deceit. My union had played me like a chess piece. For some reason, the committee head had decided for some reason that made no sense and was against the guidelines of the group I was not going to get help. There can't be any other sensible reason.

When you have a member who has paid in the sick bank, turns in paperwork that states openly it's a matter of life and death, and then finish with the state agreeing by granting the person disability, you would think it was a no brainer. Their guidelines stated that any member who had applied for disability would receive the days needed. He disagreed apparently. On every turn, there he was, mumbling some excuse as to why I was denied. Making it worse, was the president of our union, who knew me well, who should have had the courage to step in and say wait a minute, this isn't right, never did. The sense of betrayal was thick.

This injustice continued to gnaw at me over this time. I also had been placed in such a financial hole by them not filling in the gap as they were supposed to; I felt I had to do something. Maybe if I were to file suit for the money, they would come to their senses, avoid any public embarrassment, save money and just do what they should have done from the beginning. It seemed sensible. Nope, this union in its infinite ignorance would rather spend money from their legal retainer to avoid paying me. It cost me very little, and it ran its course. We came to the end, and unfortunately the deadline for a breach of contract action had expired. They had won on a technicality. I realized, for now, it is best to let that go. I don't know how they sleep at night, knowing the injustice that they had done to one of their own.

Throughout my life, I was raised in a pro – union environment. In a blue collar family, the union is looked to as a protector of the working force. When you are young, you can't imagine a case where that would ever be necessary. Unfortunately, the cases do arise.

Before starting my career as a teacher, I worked for a short while in a steel factory where the union was a very strong presence. My earlier impressions of a union were confirmed once I became a steel worker. There were very strict guidelines, by which you labored, and those guidelines would be adhered to by management or there would be immediate and decisive action.

I moved on to my teaching career. I quickly found comparing the two unions a world of difference. Everybody says it's good to be in the union for protection against lawsuits by kids or parents. I suppose there is truth to that statement. I would consider taking out your own policy to do the same thing and find the cost. Any time the union needed members to do something as a show of unity, I was right there. I remember in the first district we unfortunately were forced to strike. Nobody wanted to, and we all lost money. A few crossed the picket line, but I stood with the others for two days. In the second district, during negotiations we were asked to stand outside the administration building to show support. I did and we were all noted by administrators who made the effort. We had a very strong anti-collective bargaining movement take place in our state. We were asked to email representatives, tell people, make phone calls, etc. which I did. The measure was overturned. So folks, I am telling you this so you know I stepped up when needed and wasn't just a taker.

Now, the union appears to have lost strength. I found that a contract was very loosely written. As a result, when administration wanted to disagree on an issue, there was plenty of wiggle room. When issues would occur, I would approach the union and they would say, "Well, they can do that" and tell me the passage in the contract that was vague enough for them to do so. It seemed often we would work with every administrative request and never play hard ball with them as they did us. I won't bother to go into any more particular incidents, suffice it to say the contract was the biggest problem as a result of negotiating from a point of weakness and not strength.

One of the reasons is we are paid from taxes of the home owners in our district as many districts are paid. Administration would always claim they were broke, and nobody wanted to ask the public for any more money. It took me 25 years as a professional with two degrees and tons of training to earn 60,000 dollars. My son is in business and within 4-5 years he is in that ball park. A big irritant for me also were the dues. When I was done, dues were almost a thousand dollars a year. Why? What did we get for that?

The final point of course is the complete total failure to take care of one of their own. When I was at the end, nowhere to turn, financially in despair, all they had to do was help out from the sick bank I had paid into. They CHOSE not to do so. I want you to always remember that. The very union that I thought was there to protect left me helpless! I never understood the outrage people have for unions. Although my outrage is for different reasons, I get it now. If you are able to survive without them, you are better off. I know this will not go over well with many, but when you have no regard for a member who is at his end and struggling then I have no regard for you.

I will close this section by saying not all unions and not all union members are bad people. One guy in particular who I will call VMan is now retired. He was the only guy I found who had the strength to call things for the way they were. He was a huge asset to our local as he came to us as a regional representative from the next level. He will be missed by all those who he served.

Chapter 33

Depression

This is a section that I am sure will be met with mixed reaction. If you are like I was most of my life, depression is for weak minded people who are whiny and don't know how to handle the things in life that come at you. I felt like everybody at one time or another goes through a "down in the dumps" time in their life. Work through it, dust off, and move on. Right? Wrong!

Several years ago, my siblings and I became aware of and spoke often of the apparent depression our parents were dealing with. The old school in particular doesn't want to hear about getting help. They feel you get the help through your own work and maybe some prayer. I then noticed that when my kids were in college they seemed to go thru a bout of depression. I encouraged them to see a counselor and work thru it because as parents you always hear of the crushing cases that occur when a young person thinks they can't deal with it anymore and look as suicide as a viable option. Both of my adult siblings had been thru some troubling times with marital issues, finances, personal problems, and had their own times of breaking. Fortunately, they went for help and received it which they continue to work with every day.

I mentioned earlier in the book that I had gotten used to living in a very tense, dark, frustrated, unhappy manner that I had grown to accept as normal. In fact, it wasn't normal, but merely a shield of protection to allow for survival. So, combining all these facts, family history, and all the damage the kick me sign had done over the *years, it should have not been any surprise that I found myself in a psychiatrist's office being diagnosed with major depression/anxiety.*

At this point in your life you may be idealistic, and ready to save the world. I wish you all the best with that; I sincerely hope you can accomplish your goals. I just encourage you to keep a balance in your life. Be acutely aware of depression and anxiety. They are real, and they are forces to be reckoned with. If you have any doubt where you stand at any point with this topic, err on the side of caution. Get some help, get a work up, and find out if there is a problem. If there is, thank God you caught it. If there isn't, no harm done. I know I will spend many years getting better, working thru the damage that was done, and trying to regain my life and all the smiles, laughter, and humor that I miss. Make sure you don't have to go thru this in your life. Ironically, I recently read a study that concluded many teachers deal with depression frequently and that it often impacts the educational process of students. Go figure.

Chapter 34

Reflections, a Career Statement, and a Little Advice

As I start to draw this journey to a close, I would like to share a few thoughts, make a statement about the wonderful career of teaching, and offer some advice to young and old who either are working or will be working in this honorable field.

I can tell you without a doubt that it was quite an adventure to go thru this journey for a career. When I think back to the class the first year, the move to the inner city for the next 13 years, and the last 14 years in the inner city closer to home, it becomes a blur. Some of the best memories are the people with whom I worked over these years. It is easy to teach in an environment where there is parental support, kids strive for excellence, and you are appreciated and respected. To take on the teaching profession where little of that exists, and that quite honestly you can be in physical danger let alone emotional or mental trauma is where the real skills are needed.

I still don't understand how a kid like me, growing up in a white-bread small town, ended up spending his life teaching kids from the inner city with the most difficult challenges a kid should ever have to face. I like to think that in doing so, I was able to show them a consistent male role model who genuinely cared about them. I will say that I learned more from colleagues and time in the classroom with students then I ever had learned in college getting prepared for the field.

Sometimes the realization of what I have done with my life pertaining to my career settles in on me. Over 28 years, I am sure I have had a few thousand kids cross my path. I think of that and realize the great part about this career is that I had a chance to impact those lives with encouragement, a passion for learning, an adult friend, and some genuine appreciation for life. The seed is then watered each year by others in our field who also embrace those same ideals. In the end, hopefully we have a young person who has encountered educators who have done their job to the best of their ability and have prepared these young people for the real world that lies ahead.

Whether they find that world in the form of higher education, tech school, the military, or employment they choose, the hope is they do so with a set of skills that all teachers collaboratively take credit for instilling in them. It can be a daunting concept, but it is one you have to hold on to. If you fixate on those who refuse to learn it will eat you up inside. Even with those few, realize that although you may think they aren't learning anything, the beauty of this profession is that something is getting through, you just can't see it right now. That thought will propel you through the rough times and keep you on a steady plain. There is no greater enjoyment to be in a public place and have your name called out with enthusiasm as the young person approaches you with a smile just so you would pay attention to them again and in recognition of your relationship with them.

SINCERE ADVICE FROM A RETIRED EDUCATOR

Now if I may, I would like to share some advice. There will be some people reading this book who are making the decision to enter the world of teaching. They will be faced with what location they want to practice their skills in. Throughout this book, I have referred to urban, inner city schools, suburban, and rural. Each has its challenges in many categories. I focused the majority of the book on issues pertaining to classroom discipline, student behaviors, and administrative support. I grew up in a suburban/rural school at a time where discipline was handled in a totally different manner than it is today. My kids went thru a similar public school with outstanding academic excellence ratings on state report cards.

My entire career was spent in urban environments. I want to clarify once again this is not some kind of disparaging remark. Anytime I have referred to someone who is African American I did so feeling there was relevance to the discussion at hand that the reader would know. I am not racially motivated whatsoever. The majority of the kids I taught over my career were African American students. I base all my comments on my first hand experiences with those students and others as well. I know that I made so many solid connections with these kids; there is no issue on me personally. In fact, as the career came to a close, unfortunately we were starting to look hard at subcategories of kids, one of which was race. I highly objected to that process because my feeling is kids are kids. I always approached kids the same way. For the education system to then start telling me I need to look at subcategories like race and adjust what I was doing is unacceptable to me.

Having said all this, readers must realize that if you choose to work in the average urban environment, it is extremely challenging. You will find yourself doing things you never imagined in order to maintain order and get your job done. At times, it is exhausting, and consumes your thoughts continually. You must decide if this is the call for you. If it is, congratulations, you are greatly needed. If it isn't, don't pretend or guess, set your sights on a suburban or rural setting, and don't allow higher salaries in urban settings to persuade you. We used to call that "combat pay." The reason was there were so many turnovers yearly that the only way the districts could keep experienced teachers was to make sure they were paid a little better than most.

In the end, if this isn't what you should be doing, no money is worth the toll it will take on your life. If this is what you are supposed to be doing with your career, it will provide you with such a sense of accomplishment to know you took the tough, rough edged kids and made a difference in their lives. Not too many people are able to say that. Needless to say, this decision is one that needs careful consideration before making your choice.

Epilogue – Did the Kick Me Sign Win?

hen you first start out in your career, retirement is the furthest thing on your mind. You are young, idealistic, full of hope and energy, fresh out of college and ready to go to work with young people. Before you know it, life gets real busy. You constantly learn new things with your career. Time moves along. Suddenly, you find yourself talking with colleagues and telling them how many years you have been teaching. When you hear the number you offer, you kind of think that can't be me already! But it is you.

I remember one time when my kids were young and it was time to go back to school; they both appeared a bit sad. I thought it to be strange and asked why since they loved school so much. They simply said, "We don't like when summer is over because we don't get to see you as much." One of the greatest perks was the chance to spend every summer being with my kids and enjoying our life. Time marches on and you start to see a few grey hairs and you find yourself migrating towards people of similar age at work, since they will understand you better than the young ones just joining the field. Suddenly, you realize that the finish line is in sight and you start looking into retirement and what you are going to do with the second half of your life. It really is that simple.

Now that you have read the book, you can clearly see how I felt the kick me sign was permanently affixed to my back. There have been many personal things left out that could have provided more evidence of that fixture. I always told friends and family as I was growing up that I should write a book someday. They always encouraged me to start writing down some notes. Getting older is a little difficult sometimes. My wife asked me how can I remember all of this and yet I have a hard time sometimes remembering what happened yesterday or last week. The only conclusion I had was since I never took any notes, it must have been from the totality of the career and how it involved my entire commitment. When I tell you many new ideas came to me in the shower, it is true. From the time my day would start there, thoughts were on the work.

I will tell you this in hindsight. Balance, balance, balance. You must take care of yourself; nobody in education will. When the day comes that you leave, they will have a warm body in your place the next year and you will be a distant memory. Don't let the job consume you, maintain a balance of work, family, faith, and enjoying life. You will be happier for it.

I wished I would have had that sink in several years ago. I certainly didn't anticipate my career ending in the way it did. I received no gold watch, no going away party, no thank you; I just didn't come back the next school year. After a meltdown of epic proportion, the professionals including the good folks of STRS decided that depression/anxiety had swallowed me up and it was time for me to get away from it, get treatment, and hopefully in time get a modicum of health back.

It is a very challenging odd life I lead these days. There are many days in which I can't find the strength to get out of the house. Other days, not so bad. People thought that the depression was totally centered on work and that once I was removed from that, everything would be normal. Don't forget, it took a lot of years to get to that point, it won't be normal overnight. I continue with therapy, medicine, and a rethinking of my way of thinking. You basically reprogram yourself to get rid of a lot of negative poison and fill it with laughter and an appreciation to be alive. I am grateful it didn't bury me.

We are just coming to the end of a very harsh winter, the second one I have had not working. SADD is a miserable fact I have to deal with in my life. Seasonal affective disorder disease from a lack of sunshine and being housebound causes the existing conditions to worsen. I look forward to spring. I keep in touch with my retired pastor who has moved away. He is my spiritual advisor, and often helps me stay focused and reminds me of how God is in control. His friendship is valuable to me. My friend from the first urban district still keeps in touch with me and his loyalty as a friend is priceless. A few friends from the second district have taken the time to check in on occasion. Oddly, it's almost as if the diagnosis has sent some of them away as if I were a pariah.

I find myself overweight and sluggish. The medicine is not fun and I will have to work hard when the weather breaks to try and regain some physical health. I have begun to go to a small gym designed for middle aged and senior citizens to try and tone up. My wife has been my best friend and companion. Without her vitality, I don't know what would have happened. My parents supported me through this process as well as my sister. My distant family doesn't even know it is going on.

I find myself working on projects when the depression isn't as bad. I am reading these days. My kids are married, college graduates, working and doing well. They are only an hour away so that is a comfort. I am so thankful to God that He never left me through all of the times mentioned in the book and not mentioned. I have reason to look forward to a "good back 9" as we golfers are known to say. I love the home we have and enjoy its peace and quiet on a daily basis. I look forward to a lot of golf in the upcoming years. All in all, it has been a heckuva journey, full of twists and turns, and a few crashes. But in the end, I am still standing.

By the way, the chapter said "did the kick me sign win?" I picked up a big pair of scissors the other day and snipped that thing right off my back. It put up a big fight, but by the grace of God, I kicked its butt.

BEFORE I GO

The teaching world has changed significantly since 1985 when I began. For a very short window, it still made sense, and there was a purpose we accomplished. At some point, the politicians got way too much control. After all, it is a favorite whipping boy for elected officials since everybody is an expert. Once they took over, money became involved along with personal aspirations that clouded the real reason why we were there – kids.

Some would think I have nothing but negatives to say. I beg to differ. Go back and read some of the selections and you will see plenty of things that kept me going. I just don't like where it is heading now. The folks joining the journey now are certainly going to be challenged. I wish them all well. You are to be respected for your decisions to help kids.

It has been an interesting journey. I have a long road of recovery ahead of me. I am focused on regaining my health and enjoying a long life with my family and friends. It's hard to believe, but someday I will get a chance to be a grandpa. Wow, that's a biggie there! The "kick me" sign is off for good. I have an awful lot of golf to play. See you on the course.

AFTERWORD

On a recent drive through my hometown on the way to the dentist, I took a casual ride through the neighborhood I grew up in. I found it fascinating how everything seemed so small and crowded. What once was this sprawling block of homes, yards, and road that was used by lots of kids to run, play, argue, and fight is now this small, crowded, beat up, ugly place. Perception is interesting. I was struck by the fact how my parents should be proud for how they maintained our home and yard to where I never knew the projects was a place people looked down on. My brother ran with the jock crowd, many of who considered themselves from better families. They often demeaned him over this, and it stuck with him. It caused him a lot of issues through his growing into adulthood that he still carries with him.

The pride that was once exhibited by my parents and others then in how they took care of their property is long gone by the current home owners. I looked at our garage and remembered all the activities surrounding that structure. I drove by the field behind it where many football battles occurred. I came up on the famous spot where Rosey and her kids lived. There, a car was parked in the exact spot that my brother had his bicycle accident, striking him in the head and sending him crying home to Mom. So many memories came rushing back; I was amazed that after almost 40 years, they are still as vivid as ever before. I drove uptown and again noticed the little changes, but a lot of old places remain the same. The Sunoco gas station, the five and dime store where I made my first money on Saturdays cleaning out the rain wells of the building for $1.25. The bridge that had a spot underneath where I watched fish come up near the shore. The middle of town, where many of the original quaint shops and buildings still stand; visual memories of strength *that even a massive tornado couldn't tear down. The tornado did however manage to destroy my junior high school as well as my elementary school that I attended. The football field behind the elementary building, filled with so many memories, gone. Even the bleachers that I worked so hard to be top salesman of candy bars for a fund raiser are no longer there.*

As I was pulling out of town, I passed the old cemetery where my dad's grandfather was buried. This is the one man I have heard my dad recall fondly stories of love that affected him as a young man of 10 or 11. His grandpa died when the man was 48 years old of heart issues. A tragic car accident took his life. His body impacted on the steering wheel, striking him in the abdomen area since there were no air bags then. He walked about a mile for help, not realizing that his spleen had been lacerated, and he bled to death. It had a profound impact on his life. My dad, who never had a chance to develop his emotions thru normal interactions with his own dad, but relegated to his step dad, carried that emptiness with him all these years. He did the best he could with his own kids. He had his own way of showing love and emotion. He wasn't a touchy, huggy kind of guy. But you knew by his presence, his support at every function you were part of, his tireless efforts to provide for his family, that he was a man's man. He knew what it took to be a dad. I am proud that he found his way.

As I turned to drive back to my own home of which I am so proud to own, I was reminded of how after almost 40 years of working, I have a place that I am proud of. Compared to where I grew up, it is a "castle". Not bad for a poor boy who was taught how to work and save a dollar. All the years of struggle in the urban jungles did in fact provide a living that took care of my kids and I now live in a home that I am proud of in my retired years.

Printed in the United States
By Bookmasters